novum 🔺 pro

SERAINA SCHRAG

# IT'S OKAY

# *Not To*

# BE OKAY

novum pro

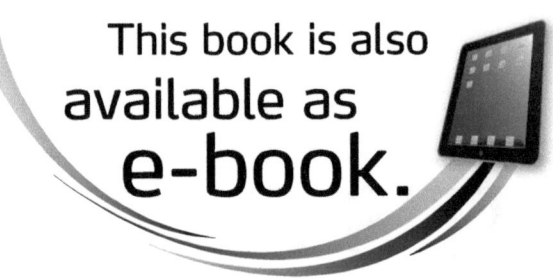

This book is also
available as
e-book.

www.novum-publishing.co.uk

© 2024 novum publishing

ISBN 978-3-99146-324-5
Editing: Samantha Acker B.A.
Cover photos: Nattanai Chimjanon,
Valerie Mercer I Dreamstime.com
Cover design, layout & typesetting:
novum publishing
Author's photo: Seraina Schrag

**www.novum-publishing.co.uk**

**Climate neutral**
Print product
ClimatePartner.com/16547-2201-1002

# CONTENTS

# CHAPTER 1

*Seven years ago ...*

... "Hyung, please—"

"Don't leave us."

"We need you."

"I need you."

"I'm nothing without you."

"**We** are nothing without you. You can't leave."

"You just can't."

Turning around, Si-woo put his bag on the floor with a sigh.

"Hanjun—"

"You're a member of B'ONE as well. Without you, we are not what we're used to being ... being the boys as one group with the teamwork and the friendship, right?"

"That's our slogan; we are who we are. We can't deny this, Si-woo."

"I'm not the right one, I'm sorry. I just can't live on like this."

Feeling his own tears in his eyes, Si-woo looked at Hanjun, the youngest member of B'ONE. He was devastated, somewhere in his own world. Suddenly, he fell to his knees, hiding his face in his palms.

"Hyung, I—, I need you."

"Please—" his words were only whispers.

Si-woo led Hanjun to his room, sitting down with him.

Lee Si-woo was the last member who joined the group B'ONE in the year 2010. Debuting with their lead single 'Find Me' in 2014, Si-woo was put in a box called 'The Visual'. His talent was ignored, and everyone just saw his handsomeness. But this faded quickly, and then people started to hate him, not even appreciating him as a human being. They described him as untalented; he took more lessons than his body could survive. The 'only' thing that would have kept him in the group was his attractiveness in the beginning, but now ...

The hate got worse and worse, and he doesn't see the point of going on. His depression kept growing, his anxiety rose. He prepared his termination letter and left it in his room where Hanjun found it.

Checking the time, it was already past midnight. Si-woo and Hanjun talked for hours and hours. And, in the end, Hanjun persuaded Si-woo to not give up and keep going. His emotional speech affected Si-woo hard, and he decided to stay with the group.

After talking with Dowoon, their manager, Si-woo would go on hiatus for an indefinite time.

\*\*\*

**Five years ago ...**

... Folding the letter silently, Jade put it next to her phone. She can't do this anymore. She trusted him, trusting him it won't happen again, but ...

... he broke his promises. He had to, as always.

Flashbacks of her childhood ran through her mind as she closed the door behind her.

*'Papa, you will come to my play today, right?' 'Of course, Sweetheart. Daddy will be there.'*

*'Papa, you will come to my singing contest, right?' 'Of course, Sweetie. Daddy will be there.'*

*'Dad, you know my graduation is tomorrow, right?' 'I'll be there, Honey. Don't worry.'*

*'I love you; you know that, right?'*

*Nodding her head slightly, Jade wiped the blood on her nose away. Of course, he loves her. That's how he shows his love toward her.*

*But the older Jade knew better. It wasn't his love toward her, neither his bad memory.*

*He hates her, uses her, breaks her.*

*She is nothing when compared to Amber, the perfect daughter.*

*Having blonde hair like him, beautiful tall, perfect curves, wonderful face. The 11 out of 10 for every guy.*

*While giving her the world, Jade got nothing but broken promises. All the time, he breaks promises as if it's his hobby, his job to do it. 'I'll be there.' 'I won't forget it.' 'I won't do it again.' 'I was just stressed; it won't happen again.'*

*Those are his favorites phrases to use.*

She can't live like this anymore. It's too hard to act like everything is all right on stage and at work. Yes, there's Junghoon ... he knows it but what does she have for him to go on? He has a family, and they're not even really friends, except you call your boss your friend. Well, Jade might not see Junghoon, in this situation, as a friend, but Junghoon definitely sees Jade as a friend. A friend who needs him because, after all of what happened with her father, she connects male people automatically with her father.

Her father promised it. He promised he wouldn't do it again. This gave Jade hope, hope to not tell anyone, neither her brother nor mother. But she should have known better.

Leaving the house quietly, she took a deep breath.

Today, it will work. Not like the times before. It will work, and she will be free. Free forever.

Crossing her legs, Jade stared at the rail track in front of her. She will be free in any minute.

01:47 ... three more minutes.

Standing up, she walked dangerously near it.

*Five, four, three, two—*

Opening her eyes, nothing happened. No, she wasn't under the train as planned. But she was under another body. Quite a heavy body. The body stood up, giving her a hand.

Wait, that 'body' belongs to a male person. Is that even possible? A male person saving her life? All men are toxic; this is not possible.

"Are you okay?" the person asked, giving her a hand, but Jade pushed the hand away, standing up on her own. "Do I look okay?"

"My name is Hyunwoo. What's yours?"

"I don't need your name, nor do you need mine."

"I—"

"I don't care," and, with that, Jade walked away back home, another suicide attempt failed.

"Jade, are you okay?"

"Huh?"

Junghoon stood up and walked toward her. "Do you want to tell me something?" He stopped in front of her desk, and his eyes changed from doll to siren. "About your late-night journey yesterday?"

The words got stuck in her throat.

"I—"

Opening his arms, his eyes softened again. Judging her won't be right, he knows this. Being by her side, that's right.

"It's okay, Jade. I'm here for you," his voice almost disappeared.

After telling Junghoon everything, Jade felt a bit better. A knock on the door interrupted their talk, and Jade wiped the tears off her face as the door opened. A tall man walked inside, bowing to show the respect before speaking up. "Hello, Mr. Park. I'm sorry for my delay."

Turning his attention to Jade, he gave her a small smile.

Hold on, she knows this man. Where did she see him before?

"Hello, Ms. Evans. I'm your new bodyguard."

And suddenly Jade remembers his face from somewhere.

"My bodyguard?" her face turned to Junghoon confused. He said, "I wanted to tell you earlier, but we got distracted and yeah," he paused for a second. "I want you to have your own bodyguard; these so-called 'fans' are getting crazy these days."

"But—

"I know, Jade. I know what he is, but he got checked several times, and I checked him myself two more times. He is fine."

"I'll wait outside. Tell me when you want to get home, Ms. Evans. I'll drive you," the new bodyguard told them, gaining their attention once again.

Waiting until he left, Jade turned back around.

"You look like you just saw a ghost, Jade. I know he is a man but—"

"He saved me yesterday."

"What—"

"He is the one who saved me yesterday, Junghoon."

"He is Hyunwoo."

***

*Four years ago...*

... hugging Si-woo tightly, Hanjun had tears in his eyes. Everyone did.

They won.

They won at the Asian Music Awards, the biggest award of the year with their latest album, *Dream Big*.

They are not losers. They are not bad singers. They've made it. They are B'ONE.

***

*Three years ago...*

... Jade's arm was covered in blood.

A knife in her hand, tears streamed down her face.

The hair: a living mess. The eyes: dark circles surrounded them. Gripping the knife tightly, her knuckles turned white. Jade looked down at herself, a total mess ...

Her hand slowly opened its tight grip, and the knife dropped to the floor. Touching her face, her lips were swollen, and blood dripped down. A few scratches around her cheek, same on the forehead.

It happened again. He promised not to, but he did.

The hope she had is not there anymore. It won't come back ever again. She lost it forever. Thinking she had lost it two years ago,

11

she hadn't. She made the mistake of letting him in again. Even after Hyunwoo and the shit she was going through. He couldn't get enough.

Upon standing up, she saw herself in the mirror. Jade broke down and didn't bother to stand up again. Her phone rang and rang but Jade ignored it. It rang a third time and a fourth time before she looked at the number. **Hyunwoo.**

Jade swiped it up and instantly heard his voice. "Jade, where are you? I know, you said you're sick, but—"

"Jade? Jade, are you there?"

"Hyunwoo ... I-, I did... it—. I did it again," she whispered. Hyunwoo grabbed his phone tighter. "I'm right there. Stay on the phone. Don't hang up."


Jade's father opened the door and, without saying a word, Hyunwoo pushed him aside and ran upstairs to Jade's room. He knocked twice ... nothing. He knocked again ... Nothing.

'Please, don't. Just don't, Jade.'

After a moment, the door opened a bit. He caught a sight of her face. It was full of bruises and blood. Hyunwoo got in and closed the door behind him. Without a second, he hugged her tightly ...

"I'm here. I won't leave you."

Jade actually accepted the whole bodyguard thing with Hyunwoo and Junghoon. He has been her bodyguard for over two years now and over the years, they've become best friends.

Looking back at herself, the younger Jade wouldn't believe it. Yes, Jade has a male best friend. Someone she trusts with her whole life.

He is one of the few men who can touch her. He was always around her and didn't hesitate to punch someone if she wasn't feeling well about being touched by them.

Hyunwoo was quite tall with broad shoulders and has a few tattoos, which made him look hot as fuck and like a badass. He was Jade's closest friend, except Hannah. Sadly, Hannah lives currently in South Korea because of her work. That's why they don't see each other that often.

Pulling away, she faced him with tears in her eyes. "Do you wanna talk about it?" Shaking her head slightly for a no, Hyunwoo understood. "You don't have to. I'm here if you wanna, though." Hugging her tightly, he brushed up and down her back.

"You know, we have to tell Junghoon," he whispered. Jade nodded, her head still on his chest. "Let's get you cleaned up and out of this house first."

"I don't want to be here any longer," she mumbled quietly.

"My place?" Giving him only a small nod, Hyunwoo patted her back slightly, but she flinched at the touch.

"I'm sorry." Jade faked a smile—

But suddenly something seemed strange. Her sight got blurry while she tried standing up, Hyunwoo caught her on time. While holding her in one arm, he pulled out his phone. —**Park Junghoon**—

Hyunwoo picked Jade gently up and walked behind Junghoon to his car. Putting her inside, he was still holding her.

Junghoon could smell the alcohol from her father's breath miles away. He had been aware of him hitting and harassing her for years now.

Her sister saw her father literally as her role model. She doesn't do 'much' but sometimes she does let her anger out on Jade.

The real problem is her father. He once tried to use her also for his personal pleasure, but, fortunately, Hyunwoo was picking up Jade at that moment and came between her and her father before he could do anything.

Jade blinked a few times to get used to the bright light on the ceiling.

Turning her head, Junghoon and Hyunwoo sat on chairs, and next to them were a lot of cups. All of them were empty, except the one in their hands. A strong coffee scent was in the air.

"Junghoon?" Jade whispered.

Junghoon sprang up and ran to her. "How are you?"

"My head hurts a lot, and I feel like a car just crashed into me."

"I'll bring you tea. Wait a second."

13

Hyunwoo sat down next to her, brushing her hair back. Flinching away, he stared at her in shock.

"Jade—"
"I'm sorry ... I said I won't do it again ... but I did."
"I'm here with you. I'll never let you alone ever again."
"... he was much ... worse this time," she mumbled through her tears.
"I think it is time you get your own house, Jade," he whispered.
"I ... I can't."
"Jade, I don't want you to get hurt anymore. It's not just them hurting you; you hurt yourself, too. If you don't want to live alone, I'll live with you. I'm your best friend."

Jade didn't answer. The door opened and Junghoon was back. He rushed Hyunwoo out of the room to talk with Jade alone. Jade sighed slightly. "... I wanna have a life again."
"I'll call someone for an apartment." He patted her hand, Jade flinched also this time. Junghoon's sight was full of anxiety. "I'm sorry," he mumbled.

Jade, half-Korean and half-British, has been living in England since her birth.
For over seven years now, she has been a very famous singer. She's also an actress for more than four years now. She started with a lead role when she was nineteen.
As soon as the movie was released, she became really popular as an actress and got many requests for main roles in other movies. She has an older brother and an older sister. Well, her parents are divorced. While her mother, a model, was living in France, Jade had been staying with her father and her older sister over the years. Her brother lives in Spain with his wife and kid; they moved away a long time ago, leaving her alone with her abusive father and sister.
She got hit by them all the time, and they used her to let their anger out. Over time, Jade got diagnosed with depression and

anxiety. At first, she didn't tell anyone until Junghoon gained her trust.

Compared to Jade's father, her sister is nothing. Because of him, Jade has trust issues with men and didn't let them touch her.

She is a professional and, for her job, she can work with male actors. She always expects the worst of them, though.

The only two men she trusts her life with are Hyunwoo, her bodyguard and best friend, and Junghoon, her boss and a very close friend.

She has a really hard time opening herself to people and trusting them. The only people who know about her situation with her family are Junghoon, her boss; Eunwoo, her makeup artist; Hyunwoo, her personal bodyguard; and her best friend, Hannah, who's currently in South Korea.

Jade has tried to commit suicide three times, but she failed each of those times. The last time she tried was the day she met Hyunwoo for the first time.

Funny story to tell your family about how you've met your best friend, right?

The bruises her father and sister gave her are marked all over her body. That's why her makeup artist always covers them up if they need to be covered.

And, as you could already imagine, she isn't quite confident, but around the right people, she is just herself.

Jade is more an introverted person than an extrovert. And sometimes it's really hard for her to act in a scene or to open up to her fans with this side, especially to male fans and actors. She doesn't really have a problem working with them; it's more that she prefers the female human over the male human.

\*\*\*

... Jade's mood lightened up a bit when she saw her brother in his car. Jake was picking her up for the family meeting.
Actually, she doesn't even want to be there. Why should she even? Her mother left her alone with her abusive father. But seeing Jake after such a long time, it was totally worth it.
Jade was currently in Spain filming the last scene of her movie, and the time was perfect for the meeting.
He drove a gray car, and his windows were open. She turned back to the other actors and said goodbye.
"We'll see you at the premiere."
Lifting her bag from the chair, she walked to her brother's car, Hyunwoo right behind her. Her brother opened the door for her and tried to hug her.
"No hug, Jake ... please."
"I'm sorry, Jade. I've just missed you very much. You good?"

Receiving a small smile, Jake took the bag from her.
"What about you? How's Amanda?"
"She's doing great. She took her first step two months ago."
"I can't wait to see her."
Turning the music, a bit louder, Jade stared through the window to the beach. Today was the last day of her new movie, *Angels of Perfections*.
Hopefully, the family meet will end on a good note.

Hyunwoo stood next to Jade while her sister and father walked inside.
"How was work?" her father asked.
Hyunwoo was already ready to do something, but her father didn't do anything. Jade didn't answer him.
She looked around, ignoring him completely — and there she is, Amber Evans.
Her ash blond hair was falling from her shoulders with perfect beach waves. Her glasses around her blue eyes made her look

very smart and, with the suit, everything matched. She was a teacher at the biggest university in England. Of course, her father likes her more than Jade. Jade was used to it and just rolled her eyes when she heard Amber.

Amber has a quite high-pitched voice, and it sucks to hear it.

"Heyy, Jade, honey, how are you?" she asked in a sweet tone, while trying to hug her.

Hyunwoo pushed her away. "No touching," he said in a low voice.

"Wow, calm down. You don't have to be rude like that. Don't you know who I am?"

Jade turned around. She heard a tiny voice screaming her name. Amanda was in her sister-in-law's arms and had a big smile on her face. She has dark curly hair like her mother, but her skin tone was a lot brighter than Isabella's. Isabella, her mother, was as beautiful as her country. She was quite tall with long dark, curly hair. She is from Spain, but she has lived in England since her third birthday. Now they decided to move back to her hometown.

"Hello, sweetie," Jade whispered.

\*\*\*

"And the winner of this year's biggest award is ..."

"... B'ONE!" the host screamed through his microphone.

The GUIDS, their fandom, started cheering, and the whole arena applauded, well, it was their fans, respectful people and the artists who actually support B'ONE.

B'ONE, is a South Korean boy band who was formed in 2010 and debuted in 2014 under QY Entertainment. The group — consisting of the ten members: Tai, Joonwoo, Yoon-Rae, Sanghoon, Jae, Kai, Si-woo, Alex, Eric, and Hanjun — co-produces and co-writes much of their own material.

The group members have personalities and roles that are distinct, eclectic, and compatible.

Over the years, B'ONE has become the world's most successful music group due to its teamwork, chemistry, and authenticity.

Their relationships with one another are based on shared values and trust.

Standing up, the group hugged each other tightly. "Let's give a big hand for them," the host added.

***

Jade was looking through her window on the plane. Right in front of her, the sky was full of white clouds. It was snowing, finally for the first time this year. She closed her eyes again and saw the face of her brother, her mother, and eventually her niece Amanda.

Jade remembered what she told Jake and her mother before she left. 'I'll come back soon. Don't worry.'

She wasn't sure if this is true. Her boss told her she will stay quite a long time in South Korea, and if she wants to stay, she can.

Jade knows how beautiful South Korea is and also that she would be away from her father and her sister, although she'd be away from her mother and Jake, too.

Well, actually they weren't always around, Jade could meet them, yes, but they didn't live with her. Jade took a deep breath and closed her eyes again. This problem could be solved before she must make her decision.

The plane landed in Incheon, South Korea.

Jade was wearing a black coat with sunglasses and a black mask. Under her coat, she was wearing a black turtleneck and some black trousers. As soon as she got off the plane, reporters and fans were everywhere. Luckily, Jade was surrounded by bodyguards. Right next to her was Hyunwoo. He walked near her, watching all the people around her. They walked past the reporters and fans. And outside the airport, a big black car waited for Jade. She jumped in and the driver drove to her company. Jade looked through the window. She saw the beautiful city of Incheon. It was covered in snow. She really enjoys looking through the window when she rides a car. There is always different scenery.

After a forty-five-minute ride in the car, Jade was at her company. She got out of the car and entered the company. While opening the door, she saw her boss was already there.

"Welcome to South Korea," he said, smiling.

Junghoon is around the age 32 but he looked like he is 21, literally. Her boss is Korean and lived in England for many years. He moved with Jade back to South Korea to his original company. He is the CEO of the big company at which Jade works. The company is called **QY Entertainment** and has lots of sub-labels. He has a wife and two kids.

"Jade!" a girl screamed by the stairs. Jade turned around and saw her best friend, Hannah. She's in the same company as Jade and is also a solo artist.

They'd actually met a long time ago but then Hannah decided to move back to South Korea and live her dream there while Jade lived her dream in England, and everything changed.

They still had contact with each other every day but seeing each other face to face is just something different.

Her new house was outside the city. Around it, there's a small neighborhood with about thirteen houses. Her house, or better, her mansion was very big and totally decorated in the style that Jade likes. She was stunned.

"Junghoon, this is too much. I don't need all of this. A little house would have been enough."

"Jade, you're a worldwide icon. This is not even half as good as you." Jade smiled with her soft eyes at him. "Let's go inside."

Junghoon showed her all the floors and also her new car. It was a gray Mercedes Benz, which definitely costs a lot of money. Jade couldn't believe it.

"I can't accept this, the whole thing here."

"Jade, it's so cute. You are so rich, but you're still such a down-to-earth person, I love this. But I said 'It's okay.' You can have all of this."

"Why do I think that this is maybe a trick of yours so I will stay in South Korea, huh?" Junghoon laughed suspiciously.

"Never."

Of course, the dressing room has to be unique, like it's for a princess.

There are so many closets, each with **lots** of clothes and shoes, as Junghoon told her.

At noon, when she arrived at a café in Seoul, Jade went inside the shop. She ordered her Iced Americano and waited for a few minutes. Finally getting her drink, she left the coffee shop.

Jade ran her hand through her hair once and walked for a couple of minutes down the street, where she soon met Kim Hanjun — the man who will completely change her whole life.

He was wearing a black outfit and a cap to hide his face from others. Hanjun even wore a black mask.

At this time, Jade didn't know that Hanjun was an idol. Hanjun was in his own world as Jade bumped into him.

Almost crashing the coffee to the floor, Hanjun caught it half a foot before everything would have ended in a disaster.

Jade was so embarrassed, trying to say sorry as much as she could, while Hanjun stood there and couldn't help but smile at her.

Normally, Jade would automatically step back as soon as a man was near her, but this time it was different. She could feel something, something coming from Hanjun. It felt like being safe and protected, but she couldn't describe the feeling, though. She has never felt it before with any men.

Hanjun looked back at his phone when he heard someone yell in Korean, "C'mon guys. I'm sure it was her. Let's go to her."

Looking up again, he saw Jade flinching at their voices as if she knew them. He stared into her eyes, confused; Jade stared into his eyes, losing herself in them. They were in a bright brown tone, like a cute coffee cup.

She came immediately back to reality after she heard the men again. "She's wearing all black, look out for her outfit."

Jade stared at Hanjun, and he stared back.

You have to be really dumb to not get the situation right now. A girl, looking like a celeb, wearing the same exact outfit these men are looking for, even with a mask, it was clear for him.

She saw a few young men, a little older than her, running toward their position. Hanjun noticed them, too. Jade glanced again at Hanjun before he did something that changed both of their lives. Hanjun is quite shy, introverted, and doesn't talk to people he doesn't know. He doesn't even like people that much, except a few. And on top of that, he doesn't like women at all. He doesn't want to have any problems caused by them. Still, he knew what to do to get rid of these men who were following Jade.

The men screamed even louder now, and Hanjun got worried. "Follow me and act normal," he said quietly.

Taking Jade's hand in his, he walked casually near a side street. Hanjun glanced back and saw the men still following them.

He pushed Jade softly against the wall, pulling her mask down. Jade stared confused at him, but Hanjun put her cap further down so you couldn't see any part of her face.

She heard the men. They were now on the same side street.

Hanjun took her hands, placed them above his neck and pulled her in for a kiss. He is definitely a good kisser.

His lips felt soft on hers and with gentle movements, he led the kiss. Oh, yes, he is a fantastic kisser. A kisser you'll never forget.

He knew exactly what he was doing. As if he knew Jade's deepest desires.

The people who know him are all sure; he doesn't like being involved with women. Then, does he like men?

Nah, like, for real.

That talent shouldn't be wasted.

Biting her lower lip gently, Jade tried keeping her moans in.

The men who were looking for her? They didn't even notice them. Looking like a regular couple, making out together on a side street, they didn't care.

Pressing his body against hers, letting her feel every muscles. Hell, yeah. Everything of his body. Caressing her waist, he pulled her against him.

A few minutes passed, and the men came back, spotting them. Jade took instantly her phone from her pocket when she saw them. She leaned with her back against the cold wall, and Hanjun faced the men without showing Jade.

The group of men kept their distance between them, and Hanjun glared at each one of them. Only two of the five men weren't Korean.

A few seconds went by, and one of the Korean men politely asked Hanjun if he saw a girl around 5' 2" anywhere around. Hanjun nodded and showed them a random direction. The men bowed at him, Hanjun bowed back, and then they started running again in the indicated direction.

He turned to Jade, and, for the first time Jade saw his whole face. The whole situation just progresses into her mind, as her hands started to shake hard, and she tried covering them up under her coat.

"Are you okay?" he asked, concerned.

Jade melted by his voice. It had something sweet and caring in it, but his voice was still quite deep and rough, she already imagined the mornings and how hot it would be, waking up to this voice. She shook her head to forget the dirty scene in her mind.

Hanjun smiled at her. He has quite white teeth and dimples, **big dimples**. Dimples which will be her complete ruin.

Hanjun just stared at her; he didn't talk as if he was frozen. "Has anyone ever told you how beautiful you are?"

Jade was totally surprised by the questions. Of course, her fans tell her all the time how beautiful she is and many men, but never in this way.

She couldn't answer, Jade just stared at him.

"And? Has anyone ever told you, Miss...?" he waited for her to finish it.

"Evans, Miss Evans."

"Miss Evans?" he completed his question in English. "An English lady, huh?"

She nodded, and he ran his hands through his hair.

God, it must be so soft. Imagine brushing through it while cuddling or even better, making out ...

"And my question?"

Yes, read the first word. 'Imagine' because this will never happen. He even ripped her out of her thoughts of **him**. Who could do that?

"To be honest, yes."

He chuckled at her answer before he started staring at her once more.

"Can me meet again?"

"What?"

"Excuse me, Miss Evans. I know we don't know each other, and it is really odd and not very nice to ask you this now ... but can we meet each other again?"

She didn't answer him. He looked at her with a smile again.

"Can I?" Hanjun asked for permission to remove her mask. She quietly nodded. Hanjun removed her mask and gasped. "Are you Jade Evans? Like **the** Jade Evans?"

Jade hesitantly nodded again. "I cannot believe it."

Jade looked up into his eyes. "What's your name?"

"My name is Hanjun. Kim Hanjun."

"Nice to meet you, Hanjun."

"So, can we meet now again, or?"

"I don't know if we should do this."

"Stop coming up with such a stupid excuse, alright?"

Jade paused for a second, putting her mask back up. "All right. We can meet again."

Jade doesn't like strangers at all, and let's not talk about men. But with Hanjun? She felt kinda protected and safe. She couldn't describe it, but she felt it, and she knew it was a good feeling. A feeling she doesn't have much and that is normally not there around men. It was different with Hanjun. She felt **different**.

"But with one condition."

"Everything."

"No one is allowed to know about it. Neither our bosses nor our friends or family. Acceptable?"

"How could I refuse something to such a beautiful woman?"

Jade blushed at his words and was glad her mask covered it up.

"I'll call you tonight, Sunshine."

Jade smiled as he typed his number into her phone. Eventually, Jade drove her car to Junghoon's office, and Hanjun was picked up by a member of his group.

Hanjun stared through the window of the car.

"What's on your mind?"

"Hm?"

"Is everything all right?"

"Yeah, don't worry."

"You can tell me if there's something bothering you."

"I know, I know."

Turning the radio louder, Hanjun's mind drifted back to Jade. Around 5'2", long brown hair that framed her face perfectly, dark brown eyes and soft lips. Her full lips have a soft pink tone. Hanjun never kissed such soft lips.

Compared to Hanjun at 6', she was quite short, but she looked cute. Styled in black, she looked hot though.

Ugh, he can't decide if he finds her hot or cute. But, Hanjun can't wait to see her again.

Remembering being with her like **what the hell**, he wants to punch himself in the face. Hanjun was never flirty with any girl or woman, even if he knows them for a long time.

How can a girl he just met make him flirty? And what's up with this stupid nickname? Sunshine, as if she would like that name!?

"Jade, there you are. How was the coffee?"

"God, it was amazing. I've never had such a good Iced Americano."

"I've told you; this café makes the best Iced Americano in Seoul."

And, like she agreed with Hanjun, no one will find out about their meet.

"What is next on my schedule?"

Junghoon looked at this watch. "He'll be here in less than five minutes."

Five minutes went by, and someone knocked at the door. A handsome Korean man walked in and bowed to them. Junghoon and Jade stood up and bowed, too, to show respect. Jade didn't feel nervous around him, which was very good if she would have to work with him.

"It's a pleasure to finally meet you," the man said with a strong Daegu accent.

"It's also nice to meet you."

"I forgot to introduce myself. I am Kang Dowoon; you can call me Mr. Kang for the beginning. I hope we will do good work together. Jade, we want you to collaborate with one of my boy groups," Dowoon spoke up.

Jade turned to Junghoon with a shocked face. "A boy group? Really?"

Jade didn't know what to say.

Is she ready to do this? Can she do this? Will she feel safe?

"It will be okay, Jade," Junghoon whispered, putting a hand on her arm.

"But—"

"Trust me, Jade. Everything will be all right."

Nodding hesitantly, she faced Dowoon again. "Sounding nice," she tried speaking in a calm voice. She knew her boss would never let a bad man with no respect near Jade; she trusted him with her life. Junghoon knew exactly what's good for her and what's not. So why not? At least, she should try it.

And to collaborate with a boy group could be an adventure for her. It would be her first collaboration ever. This could get huge.

Dowoon showed Jade on which floor of the company they'll work together. Afterward, he drove her to the members' dorm. The dorm was really big. It looked like a huge apartment but twice or even three times the real size.

Putting her shoes next to Dowoon's, Jade stood up.

"It could be possible that some members aren't here, but that shouldn't be a problem, I hope."

"Not at all."

Dowoon smiled and rang the bell.

A member of the group opened them the door. Oh boy, this man looks fine. For sure, his fans fall for his looks all the time.

He looks almost like Alex, a member of B'ONE but this can't be true. B'ONE is the biggest boy band in the world. There's no way Jade could collaborate with them. That dude probably just looks similar to Alex.

Following him inside, she saw the boys for the first time.

She couldn't move. She couldn't believe it. She is standing in the same room as them. She was right. It was Alex or is she dreaming? Are they real? Are they really the members of B'ONE? —her thoughts got cut off by their greeting.

"2, 3. Be the one and only like us. Hello, we are B'ONE."

It is real. It is not a dream. They are B'ONE. B'ONE is currently the biggest boyband in the world and, now, Jade has the honor to meet them.

"Hello, Jade. It's nice to finally meet you. I'm Joonwoo, the leader of B'ONE."

Jade gave them a smile and said hello to everyone.

"As you guys already know, you will work together with Jade. She will stay here until we are done. Then it's her decision to stay or not."

The boys smiled at Jade, and Dowoon left the dorm after he reminded them of the dinner tonight.

"Are you really Jade Evans?" a boy asked.

"Yes, I am," she answered chuckling. "Are you really the members of B'ONE?" Jade joked back, earning a few small laughs from the boys.

She still had some distance between her and the boys, but she knew she can trust Junghoon completely about his choices of men. She looked up, and her eyes met with a pair of dark brown ones. They were beautiful, surrounded by long lashes. Wondering who they belonged to, her eyes went down to his lips. Gosh, perfectly plump lips with a soft pink tone. A small smile caressed them while they were talking to someone, holding the eye contact with Jade.

"How about a game, so we will get known each other a little better," a boy said, ripping her out of her thoughts.

"Yeah, this would be nice."

One of the boys tapped next to him to show Jade she could sit there. Hesitantly she sat next to him as the game started.

Jade could remember their names quickly without any problems. How could she not? B'ONE is the most famous boy band in the world and even with ten members, all are well known: **Yoon-Rae**; big producer of the group, **Alex;** guy from London, **Joonwoo**; the leader, **Kai**; Japanese guy from Australia, **Si-woo**; the hella handsome one, **Sanghoon**; the language prince, **Eric**; the dancer, **Tai**; not fluent in Korean yet, **Jae**, the cute one, and finally **Jun**; the Maknae of the group, who usually wears black or dark clothes.

The Maknae is always the youngest of the group. Which means Jun and Tai have an age difference of six years.

And actually, there is this one guy, Yoon-Rae. He is different than the others. Better than the others. A cute, quiet guy, not sharing his thoughts with anyone. The eye contact they held, the small smiles they shared, the actions to each other ... can this actually be something?

Love at first sight, maybe?

Yoon-Rae was the one Jade felt really comfortable with.

But can this be true? Did she find the right man after so many years? Is it possible for Jade to love? And what about this Hanjun from the street? He let her feel safe and protected.

Is Yoon-Rae the same? Can he let her feel it, too?

What if Hanjun was just a flirt on the street?

With Yoon-Rae, she would work for months together with him. That would be the best time to get to know each other, right?

Why is she even thinking about that right now? She just met both. Why is she already planning her future life and kids with them?

The boys had already changed into their suits and waited in Jade's house for her to get ready.

She looked through her dresses and saw the perfect dress for today. It was a red sheath dress which fitted perfectly on her body and caressed her beautiful curves. Pairing it with white high-heeled boots and a long white coat, everything matched perfectly.

Jade looked at the clock on the wall; it was already 7:30 p.m. "Guys, we are running late."

The boys were immediately there. "Wow, you look stunning."

Waiting for Yoon-Rae's compliment, he didn't even look at her. What? Why was he so cute and nice to her at their dorm but not now? Why is he so cold? Did she do something wrong?

Straightening his tie, Si-woo opened the door for Jade and the others. "Let's go."

Suddenly, during dinner, Jade's phone rang. She checked the number; it read Hanjun. Jade almost forgot that he wanted to talk about their next meet. She excused herself and went outside. "Hello?" Hanjun said in English.

Hanjun knew Jade's fluently in Korean, everyone knows that. She isn't just a stranger from the street. She is the Jade Evans. And Hanjun? He loves the English language, and it's Jade's native language so after their moment earlier today, Hanjun decided to speak in English with her.

"Hey."

"Why did it take you so long to pick up, Sunshine? Were you staring at my handsome profile pic before you could handle to pick up?"

"No, I wasn't. But I'm sorry, I'm currently eating dinner with my boss."

"Oh, so I called at the wrong time."

"No, no, it's all right. Don't worry. It's not a big dinner, because two people are missing, so, yeah."

"Wait, that's actually funny, because I should've attended a dinner today, but my boss told me it wasn't necessary," he paused for a second. "Did I miss my chance to see you again? That's not possible, right? We weren't supposed to have dinner together. Even though I would love the idea, it cannot be true. ... It's probably just a coincidence, right?"

Jade didn't answer him.

"Sunshine?"

"Jade, are you still here?"

"Huh, uhm, yeah. I'm here, but look, I have to go now, I will text you when I have time, good?"

"Sure, enjoy yourself. I hope you'll have a good time."

"Thanks, bye." She hung up and went back inside.

What if he was right? What if he sat at the same table as her right now? Would it be possible?

Could Hanjun be one of the missing—

"Jade? You good?" Jae interrupted her thoughts.

"Actually, what is Jun's birth name, Jae?"

"Kim Hanjun, why?"

"Just because."

"Do you know him?" Eric asked promptly.

"Don't tell anyone, but I think I've met him earlier today near a coffee shop."

"Really? Cool, so you just have to meet Tai now." "Yeah, nice." Jade added with a fake smile.

It's not like she hates Hanjun. But something happened that she just can't forget. Her thoughts were on the kiss. The long passionate, but no-meaning kiss. If he was a random idol, there would be no problem, but now, she has to work with him.

And what's up with Yoon-Rae? He didn't even look at Jade at the dinner. Not once. He turned completely cold toward her. Did something happen that upset him?

Jade unlocked the door and took her shoes off. She went straight upstairs to the big bathroom. After her long shower, she dressed herself in comfortable clothes and took the elevator back to the first floor. Jade sat on her couch and texted Hanjun.

*Hello, are you awake?*

Looking at the big clock on the wall, it read 12:05 a.m. It's already past midnight, he won't be awake, Jade thought.

Getting a notification from her phone, she opened it instantly. Hanjun replied.

*Yeah, can't sleep? Wanna call?*

Jade hadn't time to answer him; her phone already rang with his name on it.

"Hey, how was your free day?"

"It was really nice especially because I've met you, Sunshine."

She smiled at his voice, "What have you done today?"

"Waiting to hear your voice again, so I can sleep peacefully."

Jade blushed at his words.

Since when does Jade like this cheesy stuff? She always hated when men were talking like this to her, but with him, everything was different. She kinda loves how he does it.

At least he is not like Yoon-Rae. Hanjun **does know** how to talk to a woman. Shaking her head to forget the thoughts about Yoon-Rae, she listened to Hanjun.

"Apart from that, not much, at least not very interesting stuff. I visited a museum and an old friend."

So, were they both so tired that it was possible that they fell asleep while still on the phone, like in the movies or TV dramas? As if it wouldn't already be a romance straight out of a book! Yes, both did fall asleep.

"Dude! Wake up. We have to go to work."

"Huh? What time is it?" Hanjun talked with Yoon-Rae in his dorm, still on the phone with Jade.

Jade woke up because she heard their conversation and rubbed her eyes.

"Who's on the phone?" Yoon-Rae asked.

Hanjun hid his phone behind his back. "No one."

"Yeah, no one. That's why you hid your phone in front of me. C'mon tell me. Who is it? Did you meet someone yesterday?" Yoon-Rae looked at him with a flirty look.

Without a second's notice, a pillow was thrown at Yoon-Rae's head. Meanwhile, on the other end of the phone call, Jade enjoyed listening to their discussion.

Learning Korean back in her early years, she has always loved it. Her mother taught Jade Korean in England, trying to bring her closer to the culture of her own mother.

Jade was smiling in her living room.

Yoon-Rae's voice sounds so good in the morning, and it doesn't seem like he was cold toward the boys—

Although, Hanjun's voice sounds even better in the morning. The little groaning pronunciation made Jade feel things she didn't know actually existed.

Getting back to the real world, she looked at the clock. It was already 7 a.m. She will be late for work.

Jade went back to the chat with Hanjun. *I have to get ready for work. See you there.*

Opening the door to the office, everyone was already there. Mr. Kang, Junghoon, and all the members of B'ONE. Seeing Yoon-Rae leaning so smooth at the wall made her heart jump a little. What the hell? What's going on?

Turning her head, she saw Hanjun. Looking like a mafia boss, sitting in his chair, he looked up at her with a smile. Her heart made another jump.

No, don't let her fall for two men straight away. This can't happen right now. This isn't some shitty love story in a book or a movie where the girl can pick between two guys.

Ripping her out of her thoughts, the boys stood up to hug Jade one by one. Jade stared at Junghoon with an anxious sight, hoping he would stop them. Junghoon did stop them.

Hanjun stared at her confused, but Jade didn't look at him.

And Yoon-Rae? Of course, he didn't give a fuck about her. He didn't even try to hug her.

"And Jade, how was your first night in South Korea?"

"Beside the fact that I almost overslept, it was amazing," Jade replied to Sanghoon.

"I have to tell you something," Mr. Kang interrupted their small talk. "We want you guys to completely focus on this collaboration."

"We will."

"We want you guys to get to know each other better, and we want you to live together until the end of the collaboration. Afterward, it's up to you if you want to stay like this or not."

"What? We should live with Jade, like in a dorm?" Yoon-Rae replied, not even a bit happy. He wasn't happy at all to share a dorm with Jade.

But why? What has she done?

"We got you a mansion in Pohang. It's around two hours away from the company, and it is near the sea," Junghoon ignored his comment before leaving the room with Dowoon.

Jade's hands started to shake slightly again, silently hoping no one would notice it. Hanjun did. He did notice it.

Glancing at her, concerned, Jade put her hands behind her back, looking up, when her eyes met his. Not again, he doesn't have to know what she's going through. His eyes gave her a soft glance, blinking from time to time, waiting for her to do something, but Jade didn't. She broke the eye contact, looking up at Joonwoo, who was still talking about the collaboration.

"Really? Why, though? I can work alone on it," she heard Yoon-Rae complaining.

What was the context behind his reaction? What did she miss?

"Yoon-Rae, it's a collaboration. I guess you know what this means."

"Joonwoo, it's also called a collaboration if she only sings in it. She doesn't have to **actually** take a part in producing the song. We are good without her. We don't need some girl from England trying to produce one of **our** songs. I want a good song."

"Yoon-Rae, that's enough," Hanjun spoke up.

He's mad. Really mad.

"We don't need **her**, Hanjun."

"We don't need **you**, Yoon-Rae, if you keep talking like this. Give her some respect, man. You're not the only one with feelings."

And, with that, Hanjun stormed out of the room.

Yoon-Rae got up, leaving the room, too.

Joonwoo looked shocked at Jade, apologizing for their behavior before following them.

"What the hell, Yoon-Rae?"

"What?"

"Yes, what?"

"What the fuck is wrong with you?"

"I did nothing wrong. All I said is true."

"Why are you so rude to Jade?"

"I just don't like her."

"Really?"

"Yeah."

"Nothing to do with your situation at home?"

"Leave them out of this."

Sanghoon took a deep breath, opening his arms slowly.

"I don't need a hug, leave me alone," Yoon-Rae replied, mad.

"Yoon-Rae, it's okay to feel hurt. It's okay to be vulnerable," And, with that, Yoon-Rae accepted his offer.


The day kinda started messed up but they still have to work together now.

The producer team split themselves into two teams.

Yoon-Rae and Jade will work on the lyrics, and Hanjun will write the music.

While Tai currently works on one of his solos, he passed the producing to the others.

If you look at the opportunity, it would be the best time to get to know Yoon-Rae.

But, after what happened today ...

Stepping into the studio of Hanjun, he looked up with a smile.

"Hello there."

"Do you already have something?" Jade spoke up after a few seconds.

She was nervous, and Hanjun could tell.

"A little, I'll show you."

Showing her his work, Jade was amazed. In such a short time, he already made a few samples for different vibes.

"What do you think?"

"Good work," she praised him.

"Thank you, Sunshine."

Blushing at his words, she turned around. He shouldn't know. It's better like this.

Leaving the room, she saw Yoon-Rae on the couch, staring at the white wall.

Taking a deep breath, she tried to hide her nervousness.

"Yoon-Rae, all good there?"

"Why do you care? I'm not here to have conversations with you, Jade. I'm here for work, nothing more," he replied coldly.

Putting his phone away, it seemed he just had a frustrating phone call.

"Can I still help with something? I'm a good—"

What's going on with Jade? Trying to help a man?

"I'm fine," he interrupted her harshly.

Yes, Jade knew, he was cold toward her and definitely doesn't like her but—? Why is he talking like that to her? She did nothing that could have actually offend him in any way.

If she had the courage, she would have definitely spoken up but unfortunately ... she doesn't.

Flinching at his tone, she looked at him in shock. What is wrong with this guy? He didn't even notice it.

Just take Hanjun. Yoon-Rae isn't good for Jade, anyway.

"I'm sorry," she mumbled, quietly, trying to breathe normally.

Hiding her hands behind her back, she walked back to Hanjun's studio. She had nowhere to go. She couldn't hide in her studio or go to Hannah. She was alone and the only person she felt a bit comfortable with just yelled at her. There's only one other person she feels comfortable with.

# CHAPTER 2

"Already back?"

"Yeah."

"All good, Sunshine?"

Nodding slightly, she placed herself in the other chair in the room. Not completely hiding her shaking, Hanjun noticed it again. Not like Yoon-Rae, to add. Not like that bitch. Is there a male version of bitch? Bastard. Such a bastard.

"Are you sure, you're good? It's the second time your hands started shaking today."

Staring into his eyes, she couldn't believe it. How did he notice? Still waiting for an answer, he looked at her with soft eyes.

"I'm good, don't worry."

"But—"

"I am good, Hanjun."

After another hour of working, Jade turned in her chair to face Hanjun.

Hanjun was still focused on the big screen in front of him, he did not notice that Jade was admiring his face.

His jaw line was prominent and could definitely cut everything within a second. It was sharp, really sharp, and well-defined along with his high cheekbones. His eyebrows are a really clean line with the perfect shape, and they made him look so hot, raising only one of them.

And then he has these eyes, you fall for them without noticing it. They are not very special with many colors; they're just brown. A wonderful bright brown, reminding her of the leaves in autumn on the trees, a cup of coffee with the perfect tone, sometimes even a brownie.

His lips were full and leaving a rose shape on his skin.

Oh god, how much Jade would give to kiss him right now, to let him take her right now on the table. How much she would give, to kiss him again. Could that kiss be better than the first one? Gosh, she'll fall hard for this man before she can think twice. But is this possible? Jade falling for a man? After what her father did?

Jade was interrupted in her thoughts.

"Are you staring at me?"

"No ...yes, I mean no," Jade looked to the door, turning red like a tomato.

"Do I look this hot to you? I mean, I know, I'm hot but—"

"No, you're not hot. I was just looking at the picture behind you."

"Yeah, right. That's why you're blushing right now and were staring at me for minutes."

"I wasn't staring at all."

"Sure, if you say so," he replied, with a smirk on his face.

\*\*\*

Being in South Korea for just three months, Jade didn't think she would fall so hard for this country. And it's not only the country she fell for. The people there really made her life better. Hanjun or Yoon-Rae was an everyday question in her head, and she still doesn't know the answer.

Hanjun was there for her, seeing every move she makes.

When she's nervous, he tries to be there for her.

When she's scared, he tries to calm her down.

He's flirty all day, but he doesn't touch her.

Although, she didn't tell him about it. He just knew it.

He saw she felt uncomfortable being touched by a man. But still, they are just friends. He didn't make any further moves for more than that. Maybe he just wants to be friends and nothing more. Maybe he is flirty with every girl he knows.

Yeah, probably.

He sees Jade as a friend.

And then, there is Yoon-Rae.

Is it true that women fall for men who don't show any interest in them? Can this be possible? Because it sure feels like Jade did.

Yoon-Rae acts like she isn't there.

Why? No idea. She did nothing wrong.

She has no idea why he doesn't like her or why he treats her so bad.

Is he in love with someone?

But that's not a point to be so cold toward her, is it?

'Cause they are collaborating. That's not dating or seeing each other. It's just work.

So, then, why?

But does she really like Yoon-Rae the same as Hanjun?

She definitely has to talk with him about it. This can't go on any longer.

She can't lose everything just because of him or Hanjun, as it's the first time she has everything. She has Hannah, Junghoon, Hyunwoo and the boys.

The boys and Jade actually got really close with each other — except Yoon-Rae.

The boys tried to talk with him, but it seemed like he didn't want to talk about Jade at all.

She hasn't given up though.

Respect for that.

Staying for Christmas brought the boys and Jade even closer together.

To be honest, she didn't miss London at all. Her new friends are here, in South Korea, with her and her father and sister both far away from her.

A new song should be aired soon with a nice dance choreography, she can't wait to show off.

Deciding to stay in Korea instead of going back to England was the best decision Jade has ever made.

Now, she has to choose her love life. It's about damn time.

She did talk with Hannah about it. She feels so good with Hanjun ... and so awkward and bad with Yoon-Rae.

Does she really want more than friendship? Or might she just search for the friend in him? 'Cause in the three months, her heart didn't make a little jump when she saw Yoon-Rae.

But Hanjun? Hell yeah, it did summersaults one after another.

Yoon-Rae, a friend? A friend she needs so much? A close friend, knowing all her secrets? One she can love without actually being in love with him? Can this be possible? But why doesn't she see it? Because of her father?

Because she already has Hyunwoo?

Because she wants more with Hanjun but won't say it?

Her feelings overwhelming her?

Not letting her think right?

She has to talk with him. With both. This can't go on any longer.

*** 

Heading back from the toilet, Jade got a picture, sent by her sister, Amber. She was trying on a wedding dress with the caption, *See you in three weeks. Single, like always, I guess?!*

Jade rolled her eyes after she read it.

"What's up, Jade?" Hannah stood up, looking at her phone. Recognizing the name, Hannah's mood changed immediately. "What did the bitch want?"

"She's going to marry in three weeks."

Jade didn't explain more and showed her the photo.

"I won't let you go to this bitch."

"I have to. After all, she is still my sister."

"However, you can't attend without a partner, can you?"

"No, I can't."

Looking at Hannah hopelessly, she put the phone away.

"I have no one to attend with. I am single, she is right."

"You could just ask Hanjun if he would go with you," she blurted out.

Would this bring her closer to him? Is it what Jade wants? True and caring love?

But Hanjun is only a friend, nothing more—

"Hanjun?" she replied, still lost in her thoughts.

"But—"

"First, he is hot."

"Second, you're around the same age."

"Third, he is still hot."

"Fourth—"

"Yes, he is hot. I know, Hannah."

"Glad you agree, but that's not the fourth point," Hannah paused and looked at Jade before ending her sentence. "Fourth, you feel safe and protected around him ..."

"... Which isn't normal with you and men, to add. Did you ever tell him?"

Jade shook her head, looking down.

"Is it because of Yoon-Rae? You talked to him. You agreed to be friends. I don't see any problem."

Indeed, Jade and Yoon-Rae talked. Finally.

Well, basically Yoon-Rae talked, and she listened.

He started with, "I want to apologize. I was rude and cold to you without a reason. To be honest, I don't know why. I was upset, and I let it out on you."

"Maybe because you didn't know me—"

"Or, because you are not close with me yet," he added.

"In the end, I want to apologize and ... and would like to be friends with you. Real friends."

It was strange. Why now? What happened to him?

But still, Jade accepted his apology. Although, something didn't seem right by the end of the conversation.

Hannah continued, "Hanjun is the best you could get."

"He sees me as a friend, nothing more."

"But you do feel safe and protected around him, don't you?"

"Yes, but—"

"Just ask him straight away. He won't say no. Trust me."

Hannah smiled at Jade before looking over her shoulder, waving at someone.

"Hanjun, could you come here for a second? Jade wants to ask you something."

Jade turned around, seeing Hanjun walking with his perfectly fine walk over to them. How is it possible to look that good in a pair of joggers and a simple white T-shirt on?

"No, I don't want to ask you anything, you can go now."

39

Running his hand through his hair, he looked down at her.

"C'mon girl. Just ask him," Hannah joined the 'conversation'.

"What do you have to ask me, Sunshine?"

Oh God, his voice. How can she be turned on by only his voice?

"Nothing, nothing. I don't have to ask you anything," stuttering with her words, she blushed.

Hannah sighed and touched her forehead before shaking her head in disbelief.

"Jade would like to ask you if you could attend the wedding of her sister as her fake boyfriend."

"Are you down?"

"Faking a relationship? I'm not the type, to do that—"

"See!? It's okay, Hanjun. You don't have to," Jade interrupted.

"I wasn't done, Sunshine."

Hannah's face lighted up, a smirk placed on her lips.

"Even though I'm not the type to do that, I would do anything for you."

"So, this is a yes, right?" Hannah asked.

Turning to Jade, he smiled. "Yes, I'll be your boyfriend, Sunshine."

"Fake boyfriend," he corrected himself.

Blushing at the nickname Hanjun stuck with, Jade thanked him.

"I'll talk with Dowoon and you with Junghoon. I'm meeting Dowoon, anyway, in two minutes," he said before walking away.

Agreeing with both bosses, Hanjun and Jade will attend several interviews in England to not be suspicious why they both left for England together.

***

"How about a few drinks to celebrate our collaboration?"

"Yes, why not," Sanghoon agreed. "Let's go to the Terrace."

The members stood up, put on their coats and went outside.

Jade was helping Joonwoo with the drinks when Yoon-Rae called her.

And again, her heart didn't make a little jump before she turned around to face him. Maybe because they talked?

Since they did, a few days passed, and they were talking with each other almost every minute. She felt comfortable with him. Comfortable with the situation. A friend she loves but not actually loves, right?

Yes, definitely.

She knew what she wants. She wants Hanjun. At least, not Yoon-Rae.

About the Hanjun part, we'll see.

"Yes?"

"I have to tell you something," said Yoon-Rae.

Looking at him, he pulled her farther away from the boys.

"I want you to meet my family."

"Your family? In like mother and father?"

"In like, my wife and son, Jade. I'm married and have a little boy. He's four. Didn't you know?"

Jade's heart stopped beating.

He has a wife?! And a son?! Why did no one tell her? Why did he not tell her?

Shaking her head, she looked back at him.

"Well, my wife is pregnant again."

"That's awesome, Yoon-Rae."

"Jade, either my wife will die after she gives birth, or she will die with my kid together. The chances are low for the baby to die but for Ae-Cha—" his voice broke down.

Jade didn't know how to respond to this. He just told her the biggest thing going on in his life. Without any hesitation, Jade pulled him gently in, patting his back. "I am here for you, okay? I will help you in any way I can. And I'll never judge you about anything."

He looked at her with tears in his eyes, "I'm so sorry for being rude to you, Jade. I'm scared to lose the love of my life, and I let it out on you."

"Yoon-Rae, it's okay."

"You are the third one to hear about it. Only Sanghoon and his girlfriend know."

"Thank you for your trust. I won't disappoint you," she said softly.

41

"When will you go to England?"

"Who told—"

He pointed to Hanjun and the members, "Hanjun is telling them at this moment."

"In three weeks."

"I want you to meet my family before, all right?"

"I would love to."

Wiping his tears away, they walked back to the members, where Joonwoo passed each of them a drink.

"Guys, guys," Eric said loudly. "I want to say something."

Everyone was looking at him and he continued, "Hanjun, don't do something stupid in England. You know what I am talking about. Do not touch Jade in any way."

"Eric, are you drunk?"

"Nope, I am completely sober. Why do you ask?" he said with a voice crack, still talking in English.

"You shouldn't drink that much. C'mon I will bring you to your room."

"So, there is still nothing going on between you and Jade, huh?" His members couldn't hold in their laughing while Hanjun tried to deny all of it. "No, we are friends. We are friends, the way you are."

"No, no, no. Hell no. You are more than we are. C'mon dude, you would be such a nice couple."

"Ha ha, no way," Hanjun still tried denying everything. But the boys didn't stop and pushed him inside to Jade, who was standing in the kitchen.

Jade was trying to reach a glass from the top but failed because she was too short. Hanjun laughed so hard that Jade turned around to face him. "How long were you standing there?"

"Just came in. Let me help you."

He walked over to her, standing right behind her and pulling her in by her waist. His veiny hand was wrapped around her waist, pulling her toward his chest. Jade could feel his abs under the shirt on her back. His other hand reached for the glass. Jade's blushing face was back, feeling butterflies in her stomach. "Blushing again, I see," he said, smirking.

42

"Why are all of you so tall, huh?" she tried to play it cool.
"Maybe you are just too short," he fired back, sticking his tongue out.

***

Wearing a basic white hoodie and some brown, tapered pants under her brown coat, she left the house.
Today, she will meet Yoon-Rae's wife and his son.
Jade told him what she felt. That she thought she was in love with him. But no longer.
She knew what she wants. She knew what she was looking for. A friend. A friend, she could tell her fears. Her struggles and flaws. And she found it. She found it in Yoon-Rae. A friend, who can help her with getting comfortable with males. A male friend.
He laughed his ass off when she told him about the feelings she had for him at first. Especially because he sees how she looks at Hanjun. He knew there was something going on, although, neither want to admit it.
But at least, Jade knows that Yoon-Rae is the friend she has been looking for. The friend she loves without actually being in love.
Yoon-Rae started the car when he saw her. They drove out of Seoul to the city where Yoon- Rae and his family lives.
"We are here," he said, smiling. He pulled the car over, and Jade got out. It was a big house in a huge neighborhood.
"Wow, it is totally your style. I love it."
"Let's go, they are waiting for us."
Yoon-Rae walked with Jade toward his house, opening the door for her.
"Welcome to my house."
"Sweetheart! We are here."
A beautiful woman appeared and kissed Yoon-Rae gently.
"How are you?" she asked him.
"Better than in the morning."
She smiled at him and turned to Jade. "Hello, I am Ae-Cha. It's nice to meet you, Jade," she spoke to her in English.
"Damn, you're pretty."

The comment printed a big smile on Ae-Cha's face. Jade handed her the bouquet of flowers she had bought earlier, and the smile on her face couldn't get any bigger.

"Is that Jade?"

Jade heard a young boy talking. Turning around, she saw a little boy, sitting on Yoon-Rae's arm.

"You must be Dae-Jung. It's nice to meet you, Dae-Jung."

"Nice to meet you, Jade," he grinned at her with a big smile.

"Wow, your English is really good. You're a fast learner, I guess."

"You are pretty. How old are you?"

"I'm 23 and you?"

"Four," he said and held up four fingers.

Jade was sitting on the floor with Dae-Jung when Yoon-Rae walked over to them.

"Do you like Aunt Jade?"

"Yes, yes, yes," he answered excitedly. Jade smiled and looked at Yoon-Rae.

"How is Ae-Cha?"

"She fell asleep on the couch. I will cook dinner now."

"Take your time," she replied softly.

"Mummy, food is ready."

Ae-Cha got up and walked hand in hand with her son and Jade to the table. Kissing Yoon-Rae softly, Dae-Jung immediately looked away.

"Ugh, they kiss so much, Aunty. I do not like it."

Jade had to laugh out loud.

"Do you kiss anyone?" he asked Jade.

"No, I don't."

"Good. Promise, you never kiss someone," he replied.

"For the moment, I do promise."

Dae-Jung had no problem speaking and understanding English as well as Korean. Sometimes he forgets a word or two, but you can understand him perfectly.

Dae-Jung fell asleep in Jade's arms after the dessert.

"I'll bring him upstairs," she said softly.

"I can do it," Ae-Cha answered.

"I'm okay. Spend some time with your husband."

Yoon-Rae smiled at her.

Standing up, Jade walked upstairs to Dae-Jung's room. Opening it, she was amazed. It was quite a big room for a four-year-old boy, but it looks amazing.

After meeting Ae-Cha and Dae-Jung today, Jade understood how Yoon-Rae was feeling. The ongoing pressure of doing something wrong, not being a great dad, the great husband that Ae-Cha needs right now, it's hard. Jade can feel this.

"I'll go now. Dae-Jung is sleeping peacefully in his bed. Thank you for tonight, Ae-Cha."

"Jade?"

"Yes?"

"Thank you."

"For what?" she replied quietly.

"For everything. It is the first time seeing him asleep before me since I was diagnosed with you-know-what."

"Ae-Cha, you can call any time, all right? Also, if you to want to spend some time with each other, I can look after Dae-Jung."

"Thank you."

A simple thank you, Jade didn't think she would need. She hasn't met anyone like Ae-Cha before. Ae-Cha is amazing. You can see **why** Yoon-Rae married her. Not only is she beautiful and caring, but she is also literally the perfect wife you could imagine. But being perfect can hurt people. It hurt Jade over the years of always being perfect. Being perfect for the image, the role model she was representing.

Seeing Ae-Cha, a mother of a four-year-old and with child, Jade only wants to help. To be there if no one else would be. Helping others, that's what Jade loves. Not wanting them to struggle like her because she knows exactly how it feels to feel like you're not good enough.

\*\*\*

Waking up by the sun on her face, Jade checked the date and time. Today, they will leave for England.

She isn't sure how she feels at the moment. Many feelings are in the air.

During the last weeks, Jade met each member's family. And yes, everyone does have someone in their life, but not everyone is revealed to the world. Their real fans accepted the fact, but some others hated it. I guess they will never learn.

She has now met Joonwoo's wife with his three kids, Kai's fiancée, Si-woo's husband and their two adopted kids, Alex's wife, Sanghoon's girlfriend, Tai's wife and their kid, Eric's wife during a video call because of her fashion show in Greece and Jae's wife and his daughter.

"Where are your suitcases, Jade?"

"Left side, upper top."

"How cold is it in England?"

"Just text your brother."

"Wait, text him please. I will go to the bathroom and get some things from there. Hopefully he will answer because of the time difference."

Almost throwing her phone at Yoon-Rae, she left the room.

Yoon-Rae texted: *Your sister wants to know if it is cold in England.*

After waiting a while, he got a message back.

*Dude, it is 3am here.*

*Why are you answering then?*

*I have my sister's notifications on loud for any emergencies.*

*That's sweet.*

*Who are you though? Are you a member of this boy group, B'ONE?*

*I am Rae ...*

After a while, he got a new text:

*Why are you on my sister's phone? Aren't you six years older than her?*

*Dude, did you just stalk me? What are you?*

*And even if there would be something going on between me and her, you can't decide about this. Just in case you didn't know, we are just good friends, really good friends. And could you please answer my question? She wants to pack her stuff for England.*

*You're right, I can't say what she can do or not ... in England, it is like a Spring start. Not very cold but also not very warm... :)*

Jade got back, and they packed together the rest for England.

"All done. I'll call Hanjun to ask what he will wear."

Hanjun's phone rang three times before he picked it up. "Sunshine?"

Jade prayed on the other side that Yoon-Rae hasn't heard the nickname because, if he did, he would tease both for the rest for their lives. Her eyes glared at him without turning her head, but it seems like he didn't hear it. He was probably playing a game on his phone.

"Hey. You done?" Hanjun heard Jade's voice.

"Yes, why?"

"Just wanna ask what you'll wear for the airport."

"Why are you not coming to my room to ask me?"

"Your room is at the end of the corridor, and the corridor is so fucking long."

"And I thought I'm lazy, but you're another level of being lazy, Sunshine."

"You would do the same."

"Still, lazy, ma Sunshine."

"I'll wear a black leather jacket, some black jeans and a black sleeveless shirt."

"You've gotta be kidding. I wanted to wear also all black."

"Let's do it then." "What?"

"Let's both wear black. We would look hella good together."

"Are you sure, this is a good idea?"

"Every idea by me is good, Sunshine." And with that, he hung up.

"We are here. Outside are a lot of fans and reporters. Walk straight to the plane with the bodyguards," a staffer told them.

Opening the door for Jade, Hanjun gave her a little smile.

He looked at her. She wore black dress pants, a black turtleneck and over the whole outfit she wore a long black coat styled with a belt on her waist. She also wore a black mask and a black cap. Suddenly, the cap became very familiar with him, and a smirk was placed on his lips.

"Looking good in my clothes, Sunshine."

***

47

# CHAPTER 3

She looked up, and their eyes got locked.

"What are you talking about? I'm not wearing any of your clothes."

"You know, though, my fans will recognize that cap, Sunshine."

"Hanjun, this is my cap," Jade started to argue with him, not wanting to lose to him.

Little does Jade know, it really is Hanjun's cap.

Jade was woken up by the staff. She looked into the face of a woman before seeing a man two years younger than Jade behind her.

"We are there in twenty minutes. I woke you up so you can change your outfit."

Smiling at her, Jade tried to remember the name of the man talking to Hanjun. It's Han-Gyeol. Han-Gyeol is the staff member who's the closest to Hanjun. Han-Gyeol was born and raised in Australia and learned English and Korean. Not only is he fluent in those two languages, he also speaks Japanese fluently.

"The cars are waiting outside. Just walk straight to them," he told them.

Jade and Hanjun got off the airplane and took the stairs down, where the reporters and fans already were waiting for them.

"Oh my god, look how handsome he is!" a fan screamed.

"Jade is also so pretty!"

"Hello, Jade!" someone yelled.

Turning around, Jade waved at the girl with a smile on her face.

"Oh my God, she waved at me!" the fan went crazy.

Jade laughed with Hanjun about the reaction of the fan.

Hanjun bent to Jade again, "If you took my clothes, you can take my bag, too, Sunshine." Letting his bag fall into Jade's arms, he ran away from her.

Some bodyguards followed him, and the others stayed with Jade. Hyunwoo took Hanjun's bag out of her hand, and she bowed thankfully. His bag was huge and extremely heavy.

***

"Jaaaaddde," Hajoon said in a cute voice.
"Jaaaaddde," Jade copied her.
Jade and Hanjun will attend their first interview together in a few hours.
Hajoon is Jade's stylist since she started her career. Walking in with a very long, navy blue dress, she hugged Jade tightly. No idea how the hug worked with the huge dress in her hand, but somehow it did. In her other hand, she held her blue heels up. "Your outfit for today. I hope you like it."
"It's amazing," Jade replied excited and hugged her again. "You are the best, thank you."
"Two minutes!" Han-Gyeol screamed, getting everyone's attention. Hanjun turned around, wearing a dark blue suit.
Glancing at her, he couldn't speak. "You look wonderful.", he then said quietly.
Han-Gyeol came toward them: "Don't forget, it is live."
"We won't do anything stupid, don't worry."
"Good." He ran his hand through his hair and went past them.

"That was perfect. Good job, guys," they got told after the interview. Jade sat down and let them do their stuff when she got a phone call. Standing up, she excused herself for a minute. "Hello!" a high-pitched voice replied after she picked up.
"Hello," Jade answered nervously.
"Sooo, when will you and your secret guest come?"
Jade didn't notice Hanjun coming through the door, and Amber asked further, still on speaker. "And your guest will be who? Some random guy you found on the street in this ugly city or what?"
Jade couldn't answer; somehow, she is right, somehow, she's not. But still, their love isn't real.

Suddenly, Hanjun took the phone out of her hand.

"No. It's me, the secret guest at your wedding. I'm her boyfriend."

"Who are— Wait, aren't you this, this Jun?"

"Hanjun, to you."

"So, Jade is with someone who works with her, huh?"

"Problem with that? Just because you couldn't pull one at your workplace doesn't mean Jade can't."

"What? Who do you think you are to talk like this to me?"

"I'm your future brother-in-law, so yeah. I'll hang up now; we have some things to do, if you know what I mean."

And, without giving Amber time to reply, he hung up and looked back at Jade.

"Thanks," Jade said quietly. "I got you, Sunshine," he replied in the same pitch, caressing her cheek gently before putting a hair behind her ear.


"Is Dae-Jung sleeping?"

"Aunty?" she heard his voice calling.

Soon after, she saw him staring at the phone with a big smile.

"I miss you very much. When are you back?"

"In two weeks, the wedding is in a few days."

"Oh, don't forget to send me a picture of you and Hanjun," Yoon-Rae interrupted the conversation between Dae-Jung and Jade.

"Why are you already awake, though?"

"My sister wants to meet me at 7 a.m. And here I am, awake at 5 a.m. to call you and then get ready."

"Bye Aunty. Mummy called me."

Giving her a big flying kiss, he ran to his mother.

"Jade?"

"Yes?"

"Are you sure this is good to keep as a secret?"

Jade knew exactly what he meant. Ae-Cha will give birth in three months and yet, no one knows about it. The members have no clue what's going on in his life.

"Yoon-Rae, if you are ready to tell them what will happen, then tell them. But if you're not, then just wait. There will be a good moment to share."

"And what if—" his voice broke down. "What if I can't tell them? If I am too scared and can't speak to them?"

"Yoon-Rae, the time will come and 'til then, your little kid stays a secret, all right?"

***

"Ready?" Hanjun asked in the car, leaving the nickname out. Jade kinda misses it, if he doesn't call her by it, but he doesn't have to know this yet, or at least, that is what Jade thinks is right.

"Not really."

"We will do amazing. You'll do amazing."

"Hanjun is right. Don't worry too much," Hyunwoo said.

Hanjun doesn't know anything about her bad relationship with her sister and father. He knows Jade doesn't like them, and they weren't nice to her when she grew up, but he knows nothing about the mistreatment. Jade is too scared to be judged by him.

Hyunwoo didn't want to push her, but he is a bit scared, him not being around her all the time. Jade assured him, though, that her father won't do anything when there are people around her, and she told him about the feeling she has around Hanjun, the safe and protected feeling.

Hyunwoo still has a hard time accepting Hanjun. He doesn't show it, but if you know it, you can clearly see it.

Hyunwoo trusts Jade without a doubt, but he is scared she might make the wrong choice in him.

She took a deep breath. "Okay, let's do it."

Hanjun got out of the car and opened the car door for Jade. Helping her out, he bent down to her.

"Give me a kiss, Sunshine."

"What? No." Jade whispered.

Hanjun looked at her before pulling her in, kissing her gently on her forehead. Both of his hand sliding down at her body, one stayed at her waist pulling her to him and the other interlock their hands. "My language?"

Jade nodded her head while she rang the doorbell, and her brother opened the door.

"Jade, I've missed you so much."

Taking a deep breath, the words left his mouth: "Can I hug you? ... Please?"

Jade nodded slightly, and Jake pushed himself into her arms, hugging her tightly.

"I missed doing this," he whispered in her ear. Receiving a smile, he faced Hanjun.

"Jake, this is Hanjun. Hanjun, my brother, Jake."

"So, you're Hanjun, huh?" "It's nice to meet you, Jake."

"Why are you with Jade together, huh? Because of her money, her looks or what? For fame?"

"Jake, stop. He's probably richer than me."

"I guess then your father is a rich CEO or what?"

"Well, yeah but—"

"I knew it. This boy is not rich, Jade. Trust me. It's all because of his father."

"Jake, don't you recognize him?"

Staring intensely at him, the reality hit him. "Oh my God. I'm so sorry, Hanjun. I didn't want to be so mean."

"It's okay. You are her overprotective brother. I've heard all about you. Don't worry."

Jake hugged him without hesitation, accepting him without another word.

Greeting everyone, the devil itself spoke up: "Jade, you're finally here. I've missed you so much."

Jade said hello quietly, but Amber didn't even look at her; her eyes were focused on Hanjun.

"So, you are Hanjun?" she asked and raised an eyebrow.

"I'd like to say, 'It's nice to meet you', but it isn't, so I'm just gonna shut my mouth," he answered calmly.

"Jade, your rooms are upstairs," Amber broke the awkward silence between the family.

"Rooms?"

"Yeah, you are friends, aren't you?"

"Excuse me, but do you think you're funny?"

"What are you talking about? She didn't say who she'll bring."

"Obviously because she didn't want to hear anyone saying stupid things about me."

"I'm sorry, Jade and Hanjun," Jake said. "I didn't know about the room thing."

"This is not your fault, Jake. It's her fault," Hanjun looked angrily at Amber.

"Love, we can have just one of them, that's no problem," Hanjun said quietly.

"One will be enough for us. Don't worry, Jake."

"I don't want to disturb but it is a quite small bed. I don't think Jade will fit on the bed with you."

"What do you mean by that, Amber?" he asked, slightly upset again.

"Nothing, nothing. You'll fit perfectly on the bed. I'll show you the room."

"Jade, how about you help father in the kitchen?"

Jade didn't move.

"You can go now," Amber said louder. Pulling Hanjun to her, Hanjun shook her off.

"Love, go to our room, I'll help your father."

Oh God, Hanjun sounds so hot in Korean. The words left his mouth so quick but still so slow.

"Thanks, honey," Jade replied only for him to hear and moved toward him and Amber.

Giving her a peck on her cheek, he walked into the kitchen while Jade couldn't hide her blush.

Amber didn't move. "You know where your room is."

Jade rolled her eyes and took their luggage to her room.

***

53

"All right, Jade I will choose your bridesmaid outfit now. Let's go to the store."

"Wish me luck," Jade whispered to Hanjun.

Not understanding what Jade just said, Amber stared at them both.

Well, too bad if she doesn't speak Korean. Her problem. She could have learned it instead of refusing it.

"I'm coming with you guys," Isabella said and also stood up. Whispering a 'thank you' to her, Isabella gave her a small smile. Turning over to face Amber, Hanjun pulled Jade at her wrist to him. "Leaving me without a kiss?" he pouted, whispering in her ear. She just stared at him. Understanding the situation, he kissed her gently on the cheek.

"Take care, darling," he mumbled.

"In which style will your wedding be? Blue, rose, gray or what?" Jade was sitting on a chair facing the window.

"Pff, you really don't know me, huh?"

"What do you except? You've never told me anything about it."

"Excuse me, I don't want to disturb, but I brought the bridesmaids dresses you requested. They're in the third room after the toilet."

"Thank you, Kim," Isabella replied to her, smiling.

Kim turned around when Jade stood up. She stopped abruptly. "Are you—"

"Hello, Kim. It's nice to meet you. I hope we'll find a good dress for me."

"Oh my God. You're really Jade Evans. I can't believe it. I've met Jade Evans."

"Let's go to the fitting room," Amber said harshly.

Still smiling at Jade, Kim went with them into the fitting room.

\*\*\*

"Daddy, where is Mummy?" Dae-Jung asking, tugging on Yoon-Rae's shirt.

"Mummy doesn't feel well. Let her sleep, Bear."

"But I want Mummy."

"Dae-Jung, I already told you, she doesn't feel well."

"I want Mummy."

The conversation of them went further, and Dae-Jung even yelled at him.

"Dae-Jung, how about we cook together for her, huh?" Yoon-Rae tried to move Dae-Jung's mind to something different.

"Oh yes. I want to cook a big meal with a lot of chocolate."

How fast a child's mood can be fixed.

Yoon-Rae faked a smile for him while they walked to the kitchen.

"Maybe for dessert, okay?"

"Okay," Dae-Jung nodded happily.

***

"Mum, you're here."

Jade's mother was the last one of the family to arrive at the house. She looked gorgeous, and her smile gave Jade a little comfort of the good old times.

"I am, and I've already met your boyfriend."

"Look, I wanted to tell—"

"I love him, and he is so handsome. Jesus Christ. I think you found the right one."

"Are you for real?"

"Yes," she answered, laughing.

"Did you find a dress, Darling?" Hanjun came from the garden to join her and her mother in the living room.

Hugging her tightly, his hands slid down her body and rest on her hips before facing Susan, Jade's mother.

"You guys can kiss each other. I have no problem at all with that. I have a husband, and we are pretty naughty sometimes, too."

"And that's something I didn't want to hear from my mum," Jade shook her head to make the dirty thoughts go away.

"Let's change and then go for a walk, all right? I want you a little on my own before the wedding," Hanjun said.

His grip tightens around her waist.

"I'll go now," her mum said, leaving them alone.

"Are you guys planning to go on a walk?" Jake asked, coming down the stairs.

"How did you—"

"I overheard your conversation with mum. And I wanna ask if Amanda and I can come with you?"

"Sure," Hanjun answered a little disappointed.

Jade pulled Hanjun by his wrist upstairs into their room. "Are you crazy? We can't have a walk with one of my family members."

"Why not?"

"Well, because we can't do the things that couples do. What if someone sees us? We'll be dead."

"Let's do all those things. No one will see us."

"I don't know. Maybe we should just say I'm not feeling well."

"Jade, we are friends. This is not a thing we can't do."

"You're right, but—"

Hanjun laid a finger on her lips. You could hear Amber talking with her husband in the corridor.

'I just don't think they are really together. I mean, look at them. Jade is crazy if she thinks she can pull this off with such a good-looking man, especially Hanjun. Have you seen this man?'

'Let's just go into her room and ask what they want for dinner. Don't cause any drama,' her husband replied.

Hanjun reacted immediately and dragged Jade to the bed. He laid Jade gently on the middle of the bed, going on top of her. Putting one of his knees between her legs, they spread automatically, and, before Jade could react, he bent down, kissing her passionately.

Feeling his hand on her back, it slipped under her shirt. With his other hand he messed her hair up and laid the hand right above the waistband of her shorts. His body is inches away from hers. Jade could feel everything of him, his breath, his heartbeat, and something of his growing.

She bit on her lips, still kissing Hanjun, which caused her to bite on Hanjun's bottom lip.

He let out a soft groan at her movement.

Jade forgot everything around her and focused on Hanjun.

Her hands moved to his hair slightly pulling on them.

Arching her back, pressing her body further against his.

Pulling away for breath, she locked eyes with him. You could see the lust in them. But there was something else in it. Might it be love?

Stripping his shirt off his upper body, Jade's eyes took in his body. Fucking hell yeah. His body, a masterpiece. Staring at it, he bent down to her.

Sometimes actions speak more than words. Right now, they did. His hand gripped the back of her neck pulling her in again.

Is he an actor or why does it feel so real? Did he study the woman's body? How to fuck good? How to leave a woman desperate for his touch? Because right now, he left her like that. His lips brushing over hers, leaving her desperate for his touch. He knows what he's doing.

Leaving wet kisses on her neck, she let out a soft moan with instant regret.

Covering her mouth with her own hand, Hanjun continued traveling from her neck to her jaw, leaving a few red spots on it. Coming back up, he finally kissed her again. Hungering over his lips, her hands left a few scars on his back.

At the same time during the whole make-out scene, which could have kept going on, Amber opened the door of their room and saw Hanjun on top of Jade.

She just stared but James closed the door immediately and excused them.

Jade was in shock, ripped out of the trance, pushing Hanjun away from her and rolled over.

"Let's change and then go for the walk."

Hanjun stopped when Jade didn't move at all. "Are you all right, Sunshine?"

She didn't say anything. "Was I too direct with this or—?"

"No, I'm just ... I'm just not feeling very well right now. Maybe it is better if I stay at home."

This isn't good. Jade felt something she shouldn't feel. She could feel her cheeks burn up again and turned away. Could this be possible, or is it just the lust they had?

But she could feel it. There was something. Something real.

He said, "Just tell me if you need anything or call—"

Jade nodded and Hanjun didn't finish the sentence.

"All right. I'll go now. But remember—"

"Remember what?"

"If there is anything bothering you, you can talk to me," he said before leaving the room.

Jade opened her eyes, facing Hanjun.

He must have come up after midnight, she didn't hear him.

Hanjun was sleeping, and their faces were almost touching each other. Her hands on top of his chest, feeling everything of him. She stared long at him and even brushed a hair out of his face, when Hanjun suddenly put his arm around her, pulling Jade's waist toward him.

Jade was shocked and tried to get out of his hug but failed. And soon after, she already fell back asleep.

After a while, Jake walked into their room and stared at them. They were still in the same position: Hanjun had Jade in his arms, and his head was in her neck.

Jake couldn't help smiling and called his mum to him.

"What do you need?" his mum asked.

He pointed at Jade and Hanjun: "It is so nice to see her finally with someone."

Susan took her phone out of her pocket and took some pics of them. "Just to tease them a little."

"Oh my God, Mum, she going to kill you."

Hanjun woke up because of their voices. Turning his head toward them, he blinked a few times.

"Watch out, so you don't wake up your girl in your arms."

"Huh?" Hanjun looked confused. Turning his head back, a smile appeared on his lips.

Jade got out of the shower and saw fresh flowers on the table next to the door. Next to the flowers was a note and Hanjun's hoodie. Did Hanjun bring her flowers? It was a whole bouquet of different flowers in every color, but they matched perfectly.

Slowly her mind came back to the note next to the bouquet.

I hope you like them <3 and put this on, it will look more realistic.

'I love them' is what Jade wants to say to him, but she won't. Instead, her mind went to his hoodie. 'That is the hoodie he wore yesterday—'

Jade put on his hoodie and went downstairs. The whole family and Hanjun sat around the dining table and ate breakfast. She walked to them and Hanjun gently pulled her by her wrist to him.

"Morning, darling. Slept well?"

"Yeah." Hanjun gave her a peck on her cheek and pulled a chair next to him.

"Thanks," she mumbled.

Jade wasn't sure how she should react to him. After everything that happened yesterday, she was confused. The make-out session felt fantastic, but did he feel the same, or was it just an act? And then the scene this morning. Laying in his arms felt so good; she felt protected, but what did he feel? And what about the flowers? Are they just for their friendship or does he want more?

But why didn't he react differently? Something definitely happened yesterday. Why did he react as if nothing happened? Why is he like that? It's always the same goddamn question, which she couldn't answer by herself.

"Jade, you ready to go?"

"I'm coming, Mum."

Taking her dress and Hanjun's suit, she ran downstairs.

Jade's father won't be at the wedding. He will probably be in a bar, drinking 'til he can't walk properly. Even though Amber is his favorite child, he still can't control himself. Amber was very sad hearing he wouldn't make it to her wedding, but she couldn't change it.

Being ready for the wedding, mentally and physically, Jade got out of the fitting room, looking for Hanjun.

Everyone, literally everyone, was staring at her as if she was the main attraction today.

Seeing Hanjun with Jake, she made her way over to them.

"Wow, you look stunning, Sunshine."

"C'mon, you don't have to say that every time you see me in a dress."

"No, Jade he's right. You look absolutely amazing," Jake interrupted without hesitation.

Giving them a small smile, she didn't know how to reply.

"Do you need me or something?"

"Why?"

"You came looking for me—"

"Oh, I just wanted to show you the dress and talk to you."

"I'll leave you guys alone," Jake said, hitting Hanjun playfully on the shoulder with a smirk before he walked away.

"I'm worrying 'bout something," Jade whispered quietly.

"About what? There's nothing to worry about."

"What if someone sees us? I mean, yes, I'm attending my sister's wedding but you, you're just a member of B'ONE, you know what I mean?"

"Don't worry. We are here in a closed venue. Everything will go well and now you should go to your sister; the ceremony starts soon."

Wanting to leave, Jade felt everyone's stare on her and Hanjun. Hanjun felt it, too.

"Jade, everyone is staring at us; you wanna do something?"

Jade pressed her lips together and stared at his lips.

With a small smile Hanjun bent down and kissed her.


"Jade, my sweetie. I've missed you so much. Give me a proper hug," an older lady almost screamed, walking through the whole hall, to get to her. She had a huge smile on her lips.

"Who's—"

"My grandmother, Rose," Jade whispered before hugging her grandmother. "Grandma, it's so nice to see you again. It's been a while."

Releasing her out of the hug, Rose caressed her face still with the same big smile on her face.

"My little Jade is back. You look very beautiful today."

"Thank you, Grandma."

Rose's eyes traveled down her body before they switched to Hanjun. "You must be her husband, right? Any pregnancy planned, any child on the way?"

# CHAPTER 4

"Let's say future husband," Hanjun gave Jade a soft glance before going on. "I'm Hanjun, nice to meet you."
"It's nice to see her with someone who fits her."
"Thanks, Mrs. ..."
"Call me Grandma Rose."
"Alright, Grandma Rose. It was lovely to meet you."
"He's very handsome ... **keep him**," she said with a wink to Jade before walking away.

***

"Jade, I need you for a second," Han-Gyeol said right after Jade and Hanjun arrived at the studio for their last interview.
It's already been a week and a half since the wedding.
"I'm coming."
Walking with Han-Gyeol to the fitting room, Jade was curious what's going on.
"What's up?"
"Junghoon called you a few times. Was your phone off?"
"I turned it off last night."
"Never mind. He called me and said I should inform you."
"All right, go on."
"You'll have to record the two songs you wrote back in 2020 as soon as you're back in South Korea because you'll go on tour next month."
"I'll go on tour next month?"
"He told me you two talked about this earlier this year."
"I'll go on tour next month," Jade repeated herself.
"Jade, are you okay?"
"Huh, yes. I'm just feeling excited to go on tour."
"Good, don't forget to call him after the interview."

Han-Gyeol walked out of the fitting room when Hajoon walked in. "Here's your outfit for the interview, call me if you need any help."

"Thanks, Hajoon."

Hajoon turned back around, hearing her sad voice made her concerned.

"You all right?"

"Yeah."

"Hey, you can talk to me."

"I'm good. Don't worry."

***

"Good morning. Slept well?"

"Yeah," she replied.

Hanjun hugged Jade shortly. "We can go straight to a café to eat breakfast and then to the airport. The clothes are packed."

"What about my airport clothes?"

"I put you something on the bed to wear," Hajoon said, while walking by with her suitcase.

"Thank you, Hajoon."

Hanjun was sitting in the car while Jade checked out with her bodyguard. Walking fast to the car, she got in with a smile.

"Where do you want to go?"

"What about the cafeteria next to the airport? I heard it should be fantastic there."

"I'm down. Let's go there."

Jade and Hanjun got out of the car with Jade's personal bodyguard. Walking behind them, Jade realized for the first time that Hyunwoo is a bit taller than Hanjun. Although, Hanjun is, in comparison to her, really tall.

Hyunwoo's outfit is completely styled in black like Jade's. She's wearing an oversized hoodie as a dress with a belt and a pair of black sneakers. Hanjun was wearing a blue jeans jacket without something under it. It shows his nice collarbones and a little bit of his abs. His jogger pants were white, same as his sneakers.

"Let's sit there, next to the window," Hanjun said. He put his sunglasses back on, so did Jade.

"What do you guys want? I'm gonna pay," Jade said and stood up.

"Nah, let me pay."

"You practically paid for everything since we got here."

After a small argument from them, Hyunwoo ended it. "I'll just pay for it."

"Hyunwoo, no, I'm gonna pay. What do you want?"

"Fine. I'll take the regular cheesecake and an iced Americano. Thank you, Jade."

"And you, Hanjun?"

"I'll take a strawberry ice cream and Sprite."

"You'll never try coffee again, am I right?"

"There's no way I'm gonna drink that ever again. It's simply disgusting."

***

"Jade, we've missed you so much," the boys said when they arrived back in the studio.

Jade had already visited Hannah and told her about **everything**. And with everything, she told her specifics about the rough make-out-in-bed session and the later wake-up scene.

"Uhm, hello? Your Maknae is back. The lovely member of your group? No one cares?"

The boys and Jade laughed while all of them greeted him.

***

Waking up in the middle of the night was something Jade often did. It was more or less normal for her to wake up at night but today, it wasn't because of the nightmares she usually gets. She was just thirsty. Sighing before opening her door, she walked downstairs as quietly as possible.

She almost dropped her glass as she felt two hands around her waist.

Putting it on the kitchen counter, she felt a head placed on her shoulder right next to her neck.

Inhaling the scent of the person, she knew that it was Hanjun. Touching his veiny hands, she turned herself in the hug around to face him.

Now, she was trying to remove his hand from her waist, but he only held it tighter.

"What are you doing?" she mumbled.

Staring at him, she saw him sweating. "Are you all right?"

"Can we just stay like this for a bit?" his voice came out as a whisper.

"What happened?"

"N-nothing."

"Hanjun, what happened?" she asked again.

"Nothing important."

Wrapping her tiny fingers around his head, she ran her hands through his messy hair. "It's okay to be scared. I'm here with you. I won't leave you."

He nodded slightly and buried his head deeper in her neck.

Jade felt his hands shaking. She knows his panic attack is about to start. What affected him so badly? What just happened a few minutes ago?

His hands start to shake first, the wide-open eyes are next before the ragged breathing follows. Afterward, he will have an outburst due to sensory overload.

"Everything is all right. Breathe with me, Hanjun."

He followed her breathing. Hanjun knew she could calm him down. She did it already once. She knows what she was doing. He feels safe with her. Concentrating on her breathing and her voice, his breathing got better. Finally, his hands stopped shaking.

"I'm here for you."

Pulling her into his embrace, he didn't let go.

"I will listen whenever you're ready."

"I thought I'd lost you forever."

"I'm right here with you. You're stuck with me even after death, Hanjun."

Hearing him chuckle, her face lit up. "See, there's the smile I love. Nightmares are not that rare. We just have to know how to face them."

Hugging her again, she buried her head in his chest, inhaling his scent.

***

A month passed while Jade recorded the songs and released the album.

She had gotten so much closer to Yoon-Rae, and, you could say, by now, they are the definition of best friends.

Jade got to the point of loving him without actually being in love. That's what he told her, too. He feels the same.

She opened up about her father and sister. About her painful life before and her flaws right now.

She also got closer to Hanjun every day and fell actually kinda in love with him.

Every time she sees him, she thinks immediately how good he would look on top of her. Reminding her of that night, in her old room, back in England.

Hannah teases her a lot about him and knows they would be perfect for each other but still, neither of them made a single move yet.

Both talked to each other a few times about very painful moments, and Jade even opened up to him about her father, finally. Telling him with words was one thing, showing him was another. The fear of scaring him with her bruises was in Jade's head every day.

Another day passed, and she was lying in bed, thinking of his reaction. How would he react? The first time she told him about her father, he threw a tantrum. Jade had trouble calming him down.

"Can't sleep?" Jade said when she noticed Hanjun on the terrace.

"Hm, what about you?"

"Nightmare?"

"Yeah."

"Your father?"

"Mhm."

Jade walked with a glass over to Hanjun.

He sat on the couch next to the pool and patted next to him. Smiling, she sat down.

They didn't talk for minutes and enjoyed the company of the other person when Jade suddenly broke the silence.

"You know, there's actually something I wanted to tell you."

"Hm?" he answered softly.

Breathing slowly, she looked back at him.

She felt ready, ready to tell him more about her past. About herself and how she was then.

Putting his hand on top of hers, he didn't say anything.

That were a lot of true words coming out of her mouth.

But was it worth it? Telling him? Won't he be scared and run away? Knowing all her past self? Her true self? The way her father treated her, her suicide attempts. Everything that happened the past years— what if he just doesn't care?

"You are enough, Jade. You are more than enough. Trust me," he whispered, brushing the tear on her cheek away.

"Thank you for opening up to me," he mumbled in her ear before pulling her gently to him, hugging her tightly. "Let's sleep. You have a big day tomorrow," he said softly.

"Ready?"

"Yeah, I can't wait to see my fans."

"Neverland has missed you so much. I was on Twitter today, and they are really excited to see you on stage again."

"Soundcheck starts now," a staff member told Jade.

Walking on stage, Jade admired her fans. It's been so long since she last saw them live.

"Let's go," she screamed through the mic.

Jade was wearing an oversized light blue pajama. It was the merch designed by B'ONE's member Eric.

The fans went crazy when she started to sing a few songs to check if everything was all right.

"Byyye, I love you," she said and went off the stage with the help of Hyunwoo.

Everything was dark when Jade appeared on stage. Wearing a bright outfit, she started with a powerful song, and after a few songs she greeted all of them.

During her speech, someone screamed her name out loud, and Jade imitated the person in a high-pitched voice— the whole stadium laughed.

***

It was the last concert of the tour. Jade was already tired in the break section. She nearly got enough air.

"Jade, slow down. It is only a concert, and Neverland will understand it if you just end it now."

"No, I want to give them a good concert. This is the last concert of the tour, please. I want to go out there."

"Jade, you didn't eat for two days because of this concert. You're not in a good condition to do this."

"What? Jade, why didn't you tell me?"

"I just wanted to lose some weight for my look, so I won't look that puffy and fat during the concert."

"Jade, you know, you have to talk about this with me," Junghoon was upset and stared at the wall.

"Five minutes before she's up," a staff member told them.

Jade's hand trembled a little, hiding it behind her back, she hoped no one saw it.

"I can't let you go on stage like that, I'm sorry."

"No-... please, they deserve a good concert."

"Jade, look at you. You're going to break down on stage."

"No… I—, I can do this, please. I want … to go out there.", she said quietly.

Junghoon turned around to face a female staff member.

"We can't change her mind, but we can change the program a little. She's not allowed to be alone on stage. The choreography always needs a background dancer, all right? And there should be enough water bottles."

"Let's do this."

"Jade, let me help you," Hyunwoo said and carried her to the stage.

"Up in three, two, one and go," a staffer yelled.

Jade was on the platform which brings her up on stage. Trying her best to cover up her pain, to look good for her fans, was hard for Jade. But still, she won't go off the stage before the concert has officially ended.

"Thanks, Japan. It was an amazing concert. I love you, Neverland," she said in her mic.

Standing on the platform that brings her from the middle of the stage backward, she tried to breathe normally. As soon as the fans couldn't see her anymore, Jade leaned against the wall. Her head hurt so much, and she could barely breathe.

A few staffers already surrounded her as Hyunwoo caught her before she fell off the platform. Her eyes closed immediately, and the staff gave her extra oxygen.

"Put her on the bed, the doctor will be here in a minute," Junghoon said, stressed.

Hyunwoo stood next to Jade holding her hand. "C'mon, Jade. Wake up."

***

Jade woke up a few hours ago.

Walking into the room, Hanjun saw her on the bed.

He looked mad.

Well, mad isn't the right word for it.

He looked **hella mad** with a strong emphasis on **hell**.

Closing the door behind him, he walked toward Jade.

"How do you feel?"

"I'm all right. Don't worry."

"Are you sure? Do you need water or food or-"

"Hanjun, I said I'm good," she faked a smile.

"You fainted. You're not good."

"I'm going for a walk," Hyunwoo disturbed them, leaving the room.

"You should cover yourself more; you'll catch a cold."

"Hanjun, I'm good. Stop worrying."

He sent her an annoyed look.

"Oh, stop it. Are you mad?"

Rolling his eyes, he crossed his arms. "I'm not mad." Hanjun leaned back in the chair he was sitting in.

"Oh really?" Jade sent him an annoyed glance as she folded her arms.

"The whole thing you did was a stupid dangerous act."

"What do you mean?"

"You've starved yourself. You fainted due to it. This is not good. You can't do this."

"But you can do this? Of course. You can force yourself not to eat but I'm not allowed?"

He stood up, "But you got hurt! You are currently in a hospital. You don't care about yourself. You care about us and your fans but not about yourself!" he started yelling at her.

"I care about myself almost over anyone!"

Hanjun moved closer to her, "No, you don't. You would throw yourself into the flames without considering whether you might get hurt! You only think about the end goal, and that is a stupid way of thinking."

"Don't you think I know this?" Jade started to yell as well. "Don't you think I know how bad this is? Do you really think I don't know what I did?" she lowered her voice to intimidate him.

"I'm being serious — you fainted. What if no one has been around you?" he threw his arms toward the closed hospital door.

"I don't need you to save or protect me. If you think it's that bad, why didn't you call?"

"Why didn't I call? Why didn't I call? Do you want to know the **fucking reason**? Because no one fucking told me! I had to figure it out by myself. I was so fucking worried, and no one gave an answer!"

"Now it is my fault for not telling you?"

He let out a dry laugh. "I don't think like this about you, and this is exactly my point. How could you act like nothing happened? Everyone knew it. **Everyone**, Jade. **Except me**."

"Oh, I'm sorry! My dearest apologizes for not telling Mr. Kim."

"Did I know the boys wouldn't tell you? No! So, **shut the fuck up**, Hanjun," she said the last few words slower and louder. Jade threw her hands up and stood up from her bed. Suddenly she felt a bit lightheaded, and her vision was spotty. Her knees felt weak, but she was able to keep herself up.

"See? You're not okay. You're dizzy!"

"I'm good," she repeated herself.

"That's my whole point. You **don't want** me to worry about you!"

"I don't want anyone to worry about me because I don't need anyone worrying about me! At the end of the day, no one is gonna be there for me other than myself."

He let out another dry chuckle. "Why won't you let anyone care about you! Jade, please. Let me be this person. We talked about so many painful things. I want to make sure you're all right," he turned away, and the yelling was getting progressively louder.

"Oh, c'mon! Just because I've been vulnerable with you doesn't mean you have to feel bad like I'm a weak baby, Hanjun."

She stepped up to him, getting closer as he looked at her with his angry eyes.

"Stop treating me like I'm gonna break! I' m not a fucking baby."

Turning away and facing the bed, he scoffed, "You just don't give a fuck about people's feelings, do you? Just because your father doesn't care about you doesn't mean you should treat others the way he treats you. That's your worst trait, Jade."

Jade laughed sarcastically. "You actually think I give a fuck about what you're saying to me? Or your stupid opinion?" she yelled back at him.

Rage had filled up her body, and she can't seem to control it. He stepped closer to her, and Jade slowly stepped backward.

"Oh, but you do give a fuck! You care about what I have to say!" She raised her eyebrows at him. Did he know? Did he know her biggest secret of all? But how? Was she too obvious? "Oh, really and why's that?" she asked while folding her arms.

He smirked. "Because I know how I make your body feel. You would love to fuck me, wouldn't you?" his tone is low and full of lust. She tilted her head and a smirk appeared on his lips. Jade scoffed at him, "Oh, fuck off, Hanjun. You're so full of yourself."

Walking away she turned as she made it to her bed. She didn't mean it, but she knew it would get him upset. He just stared at her with mad eyes.

Jade stood back up and walked to him, and as she gets close to his face, she tried to stand as tall as she could without giving in and slapping him. "I fucking hate you, Hanjun. You are a fucking prick!" She turned away from him, walking toward the window. "Well, I hate you, too, Jade. Did you ever take that into consideration?" Scoffing at him, she turned around at the sight of him. He's full of anger, and so was Jade. Her breathing was heavy, she unclenched her fists and tried to calm herself down.

But suddenly he looked at her, and then his eyes looked to the ground as if he was in deep thoughts. "Fuck it."

Speeding his way over to Jade, he grabbed her face, leaning down, before smashing his lips onto hers. Jade melted into the kiss, placing her hands on his wrists, her body filled with heat, and her stomach filled with butterflies.

The rage in her body was still there, but warmth had been added. He backed up a bit, their lips still connected, and they fell on top of the bed.

"I hate you so fucking much; you drive me insane," he spoke in between kisses. His hands find her waist and her legs straddled over his.

"I fucking hate you, too; you get me so fucking aggravated," as her hands find his face and the simple kiss turns into a make-out. A **rough** make-out.

He moved his hands to her ass, and he squeezed just a little, making her laugh a bit. Pressing herself down, grinding onto his lap, he let out a groan.

The friction made her let out a quiet moan, and his tongue slipped into her mouth. His hand trailed her body, and she could feel him getting hard.

"Damn," he laughed a little. They were both breathless from the absolute heated make-out session.

"Oh, shut up, Hanjun."

Gently grabbing her chin, he kissed her again before pulling away, "I don't hate you, Jade. I was just mad." He stared into her eyes as she smiled.

"I'm sorry. I don't hate you either, and I'm sorry for calling you a prick and not telling you what happened."

"Oh so, I'm full of myself, then?"

Still laughing, she pulled him into another kiss.

Jade just stepped out of the shower when she heard a knock. "Just a second."

Closing the door behind her, Hannah walked up to Jade's bed. "Girl, you gotta promise not to be loud."

Hannah tilted her head in confusion. "Okay," she hesitated as Jade laid next to her.

"So, Hanjun and I were arguing ..."

"I said some quite nasty things ..."

"He said some quite nasty things ..."

"We both said we hated each other, and then we ended up having a very rough heated angry make out."

Her eyes widened and her mouth opened, Jade handed her a pillow. Grabbing it, she screamed into it loudly, and Jade laughed a bit. She was surprised by the quick emotion change Hannah did as she removed her face from the pillow and rapidly hit Jade with it.

"I told you," her voice is a loud whisper.

"You're telling me fucking everything."

"Okay, all right. But enough with the pillow."
"How did you guys initiate the kiss?" she lightly hit Jade out of excitement.

A few days later, Jade could go home.
Hanjun and she didn't talk about their make-out since it happened. Being not even once alone with him in the hospital after it, she felt weird.
Is he ignoring her? Jade wasn't sure what she feels or even more what **he** feels. Does he feel the same? Would he actually choose her over any girl he could have? Or, will she just be a flirt before someone else would come? The collaboration-flirt? Or, does he really want her that much?

*** 

Jade couldn't sleep again and walked outside. She saw Hanjun at their usual spot, the couch.
Passing the pool, she made her way over to him.
"Nice seeing you here again on this beautiful night, Sunshine," he looked at her and smiled.
Jade blushed at his words, praying he wouldn't see it. She overplayed her blush with a smile and sat down next to him.
"Did you miss your bed?"
"Oh, how sweet you're worried about me." Jade smiled at him when he placed his hand on her thigh.
"Do I?" he lowered his voice.
She tensed up for a second but let it go.
"Well, tell me."
"Tell you what, Sunshine?"
"About our little argument. Didn't you like it, Hanjun?" she said, smirking.
With a small chuckle, she removed his hand off her thigh.
"Well, I don't like to argue with you," he tilted his head and placed his hand back on her thigh. "But I have to confess, I did like it this time."

"Specifically, **the end** of it."

Jade could feel the pool between her legs forming in her underwear as his hand gripped a little. Getting closer to him, his eyes automatically fell to her lips.

He leaned forward, grabbed her face and kissed her. Her hands dropped to his wrists, kissing him back. The kiss deepened, and she pushed him forward to sit on his lap.

He was looking at her in a way she has never seen on him or any men before.

It was not lust right now. It was a caring stare. As if he would want to make sure she felt comfortable.

She started caressing his face, gripping his hair, feeling his whole face.

Giving him wet kisses on his jaw before kissing up to his lips, he let out a groan, gripping her waist, pushing her against him. A smile appeared on his lips before he made his next move. He had her approval. She wants it. Pinning her down to the couch, Jade wrapped her legs around his torso as his hands trailed her body. His hands gripped her waist tightly, and her hands are back in his hair. Arching her back, she felt him getting hard. Hanjun let out a groan, and she slipped her tongue into his mouth.

In one swift movement, he picked her up, breaking the kiss and placing her on his lap so her back hit his chest.

A chuckle left her mouth as he placed wet kisses on her jaw and trailing down to her neck. His hand moved down just before her waistband of her shorts.

"Are you sure?"

"Yes."

"Tell me to stop if you're uncomfortable."

Jade leaned her head back on his shoulder.

Staying like this for a few minutes, Hanjun kissed her neck gently. "Let's get you cleaned up."

Jade stood up with her knees still shaking a bit.

"Need any help?"

She rolled her eyes at him. "I'm good."

Walking upstairs to Hanjun's room, Hanjun put his hand to the small of her back.

In the room, Jade headed to the connected bathroom. "I'll clean myself up. It's okay."

He smiled. "You sure?"

She just nodded, and Hanjun walked away.

Jade wasn't ready yet to let him see the bruises on her body ... her past self, the destroyed one.

Scared of what he could think, leading her not to show him. Telling him is still different than showing him.

She cleaned herself up and washed her hands before leaving the bathroom.

Scrolling through his phone, he lifted his head when he heard Jade. "I'll go to my room now."

"Already?" he pouted.

"The boys would notice it," she replied quietly. "We can't risk it."

Jade was already at the door when Hanjun jumped off the bed. "Jade, wait."

She turned around. "Yes?"

He took a deep breath but then— "Nothing ... just sleep well."

"Thanks, you too."

\*\*\*

"You don't think I know how **bad** it is? Not only for me but for her? How **wrong** it is?"

"I know, okay? I know that it's bad and wrong and stupid and ignorant, but I can't change it."

"I tried. I fucking tried so many times, but I can't handle it."

"I can't let her feel as if she is nothing to me because she means the world to me. I just want her and no one else. Please, I can't change it and I don't want to change it either."

"I want her to be mine and only mine."

"Hanjun, I know what you feel and in which state you are currently, but please let me tell you, it won't be easy. Neither for you nor for her."

"It will be harder than with any of the boys. Before you do anything, think about it and think about her too."

"You deserve to be happy and she does, too. If that is what makes you happy, then it's the right choice, if not, you know what you have to do."

With hesitation Hanjun nodded, and Yoon-Rae left the room.

Jade had hidden herself in a room next to the kitchen. She overheard the whole conversation. Still not sure if Hanjun meant Jade, she opened the door after Yoon-Rae passed it. Walking to the kitchen, she tried acting like nothing happened.

"Jade?"

"Yeah?"

Jade turned around to face him. She put the knife for cutting the strawberries away, looking at him.

"Uhh, nothing. Sorry."

What's wrong with him these days? He keeps trying to tell something but then stopping himself.

She shrugged her shoulders, turning back around.

"Uhm, no wait. You know what?"

"What?" she answered, chuckling.

"I like you," he blurted out.

She almost dropped the knife while turning back around.

"I mean, I like you a lot. Not just as a friend. I like you **more** than a friend. I fell in love with you when we first met. I know, we've only known each other for a few months, and this could ruin our friendship. I know all of it. But my question is, could we try it? Do you think we could try to go out together?"

"Hanjun, I—"

"Stop," he laid a finger on her lips. "I know this sounds cheesy, stupid, and straight out of a romance story, but I will wait for you. You've been through a lot, and I do understand if you need time, just know, I will be here, waiting for you."

Since the day Hanjun confessed, he didn't push her at all. As he said, he will wait for her. For her to be ready, fully convinced about it. But, honestly, Jade couldn't wait any longer.

She wasn't fully ready yet, but she wants him, she needs him. Closing the door behind her, she walked quietly through the corridor to the kitchen. Putting her big bag down, she looked up. Hanjun was on their couch outside, alone.

A smile appeared on her lips while she opened the big window. Hearing someone coming, Hanjun turned around.

Jade froze in her walk.

His eyes were locked with hers, not leaving her once. Walking toward him, sitting down, he smiled at her, before his gaze wandered to her lips.

"Remember the last time we were out here?"

Staring back into her eyes, a smirk appeared on his lips. "It's quite vague. You might have to remind me, Sunshine."

Rolling her eyes, she chewed on her bottom lip, moving closer to him. "Do I really?" her voice had a sense of amusement in it. She climbed on top of his lap, straddling his legs.

"You definitely have to remind me."

Jade smiled and leaned in for a kiss. Her hands wandering to his neck, through his hair, pulling on them gently.

Kissing his jaw, her hands didn't leave his hair once.

"Last time you made me feel so good," her lips traveled down his neck before it went back to kiss along his jaw, leaving wet kisses all over it.

Jade grinded down a little and started to feel him grow hard. Breaking the kiss, she stared into his eyes.

Hanjun smiled and pulled her back. This time, the kiss was filled with much more hunger and desire. His lips moved down to her neck caused her to grind against him more and a groan left his mouth, not caring if anyone could hear them.

"I missed this," his words made her smile.

"I did, too."

Guiding her to grind against him more, his hands stayed on her hips. Not leaving his lips, the friction caused them to moan quietly into each other's mouths.

Caressing her hips, his hands traveled higher, gripping on her thighs before moving up further.

Her hand touched his and without a word, he stopped. Pulling away, their faces were inches apart.

Hearing each other's heartbeat, he kissed her forehead. She wanted to speak up, but a finger was laid on her lips while he shook his head. "I know. It's okay. Don't worry. We don't have to go this fast."

"I don't wanna go too fast," she said as if she didn't hear him.

Nodding, he put his hands on her face. "That's all right. You've been through a lot. I will wait for you."

Faking a smile, Jade looked up. "I'm sorry," she lowered her head back.

"Sorry for what?"

"For not being ready yet."

His face contorted to a confused look. "Why would I be mad about it?"

"Well, I—"

"Take the time you need. I'm okay with that. You just gotta tell me whenever I make you uncomfortable."

Biting her bottom lip, she replied with a small okay.

"Do you wanna know why I stopped you?" her voice whispered.

"I don't need an explanation, Jade."

Letting her hands drop to his, she caressed his wrists gently. "I want you to know."

His hands traveled from her waist back up her body. Touching every single part of her, leaving her assured, it's all right.

Ending by her neck, his hands slowly gripped it from behind, caressing it softly.

Feeling his fingers behind her ears, stroking her skin with soft movements, almost made her tear up.

Running his hands through her hair right behind her ears, kissing her forehead again, left her reassured. It had no sexual meaning in it. It was a way of showing love and trust.

"Tell me," the volume of his voice changed to match hers.

His fingers were still on her skin, stroking it gently, not breaking eye contact.

# CHAPTER 5

"Because, because this makes me feel something. You make me feel something. You make me feel safe and protected. I don't want to lose this feeling."
Interlocking his fingers with hers, he smiled.
Looking down at their hands, his thumb stroke hers.
"I don't want to lose this either, Jade. You know this."
"I like this."
**"I like you, Hanjun."**
Placing a quick kiss on his lips to distract herself from what she just said, she started to blush.
Smoothly, Hanjun let her hands go, grabbing her head gently and pulled her in for another kiss.

***

Three months ago, Jade and Hanjun got together. No one except Hannah knew something about them. Well, Yoon-Rae did know about the feelings both have but they didn't tell him straight face to face about their relationship.
Jade feels bad for not telling him. He is also her best friend. They tell each other everything, but Hanjun and Jade agreed on a secret relationship, so it stays as a secret even if it breaks Jade's heart to not tell Yoon-Rae.
Seeing him every day without telling him about Hanjun makes her feel bad as best friend. Several times, she almost blurted it out. She thinks he knows it, but she didn't break the rule. If he finds it out by himself, everything is all right.

***

A phone call interrupted Jade and her friend talking.
"I'm sorry, wait a second."

"Hello?"

"Hi, can you come to the parking lot?"

"Uhm, are you here?"

"Yes, Love. I'm waiting, can you come out now?"

"I'm in school, I can't just leave," she replied, hoping her friend doesn't listen to the conversation.

Glancing over, her friend is already flirting with a boy next to her.

"You're sitting in the cafeteria, Darling, and your next lesson is in two hours. This is enough time to see your loved one, no?"

Jade thought for a second, "All right. Anything else to say?"

"Come here now. I miss you."

—and with that, he hung up.

Jade chuckled before putting the phone back.

"Who was that?"

"Just a friend."

Jade stood up, packing her stuff.

"And where are you going, Miss?"

"My next lesson is in two hours. I'm going for a walk. See ya."

"Take care."

Jade opened the door, walking out of the school. She watched out for Hanjun's car. You can't fail to see his car; it was an expensive black Mercedes-Benz.

She smiled when she saw him leaning on the passenger door. Standing there like a mafia boss, he looked so hot. Staring at his phone while running his hand through his hair. Ugh, so sexy. A flower bouquet in his left hand led Jade to melt as soon as she saw it.

Hanjun still likes to give Jade small gifts all the time, especially flowers. And right now, he got her flowers. A beautiful bouquet of different kinds of tulips.

"H—" Jade couldn't finish her greeting; she was already cut off by Hanjun's lips on hers. He put his cap further down, hiding his face under it. You couldn't see who he was and neither what they did.

While pulling her toward him, he opened the car door, letting them fall into it. She was on top of him, her hands on his hard chest.

He bit gently on her lower lip, causing her to moan quietly. Hanjun took his opportunity and slid his tongue into her mouth.

"Hi," he smiled once they pulled away. "I've missed you, my Love."

"These are for you," he said, handing her the flowers. He gave her a peck on the lips, not giving her a chance to say hello.

"What if someone—"

"The windows are tinted, and the door is closed. No one could."

***

Hanjun texted Jade: *Love, can I come over later to your house? Don't wanna drive home two hours to be at the mansion ...*

*Uhm, you can't ... I'm meeting someone today, and I'll go to bed early. I'm sorry, maybe another day.*

*—Can I just come to sleep with you? You know what I mean, I would love to wake up next to you <3*

*You've got my keys.*

"Aunty Jaddde," Dae-Jung greeted her.

"Welcome to my house, Dae-Jung."

"Thanks for watching him," Yoon-Rae said.

"No problem, I love to do this. You can bring him anytime. Make yourself a nice evening with Ae-Cha."

"We will," Yoon-Rae hugged Jade tightly before he left Dae-Jung at her house and walked back to his car.

He still doesn't know it. She wants him to be the first one to know but what if Hanjun doesn't want it? She can't lie to him any longer. It's too hard.

Jade woke up to an empty bed. The boys were up earlier than her. She scratched her head, rubbing her eyes.

Hearing loud music from downstairs, two guys were easily heard singing the wrong lyrics and she couldn't help chuckling.

After a few minutes, Jade got downstairs.

"Hello, my Lady," Hanjun and Dae-Jung greeted her. Both bowed at her and laughed afterward.

"Hello, dear Gentlemen," she replied.

Jade walked past Dae-Jung and Hanjun to get the dishes for breakfast but failed because Hanjun pulled her toward him. Hugging her tightly, he gave her a peck on her forehead. "Slept well?"

"Yeah."

"Why didn't you tell me you dyed your hair?"

"Do you like it?"

"Yeah, red does always look good and sexy."

"I know," he answered, smirking.

"Eww, stop it," Dae-Jung pulled on Hanjun's jogger pants.

Eventually Jade noticed that Hanjun wasn't wearing a shirt. His jogger pants were hanging so low on his waist you could see his hot abs and his V-line.

"Yah, put something on," Jade said and walked away. Hanjun ran after her, catching her and pulled her on his chest. "You know, it's hot how you use Korean and English words in one sentence," he whispered in her ear.

"What do you mean?"

"I like the sound of 'yah'. It sounds good. Kinda more badass."

Placing her hands on his chest, her eyes were filled with concern. "We need to talk."

"Did I do anything wrong?"

Shaking her head, she pulled him into a hug. "I can't lie any longer to Yoon-Rae. It's not fair to not tell him."

"It's all right, Love. You can tell him."

With a matching pastel purple hoodie and jogger pants, white shoes and a white hat, Jade walked downstairs. Next to her, Dae-Jung in full blue with the same outfit in a small size.

Hanjun was wearing a shirt and a black leather jacket over it. His trousers were also black. Hanjun's outfit matched perfectly with his new hair. How can he be so hot? Like what the hell? How is it possible to rock every single outfit he is wearing?

Meeting Yoon-Rae as soon as possible after talking to Hanjun, he wasn't shocked nor surprised at all.

"I knew it."

"I saw you looking at each other and talking when no one was watching."

"I'm glad you found someone you can trust, Jade."

"Still, be careful. It won't be easy. There is a lot of hate in this world."

\*\*\*

Hearing a knock, Hanjun still faced the wall of the shower.

"Darling? Are you okay?"

Jade didn't reply.

"Darling? Do you need any help? Did something happen?"

"Can I join?" her voice came out as a whisper.

Huh? Jade wants to shower with him. Letting him see her body for the first time.

"I would love it," he whispered back.

When her two tiny arms wrapped around his waist, Hanjun turned around. He kept his eyes closed; she might still feel uncomfortable. Hearing her breathing stronger, he kept his eyes closed.

"I'm not gonna open them until you're comfortable," he assured her. His hands reached for hers, letting her feel his body. Feeling his broad shoulders, his muscular chest, down his abs to his waist. Not leaving a single part of his body out, she touched it all.

His eyes were still closed, enjoying it all. She has never touched him like this at all. Gentle but risky.

Coming back to his neck, her finger scratched down it, leaving some red scratches behind. Groaning at her touch, she felt his hands on her waist pulling her near him.

Her hands left his neck and traveled down his body once again before taking them away from him. Taking his hands in hers, he squeezed them softly and leaving his on her body, her hands fell back down.

First, he didn't move them at all. He rested them on her lower waist, right next to her ass. Slowly, they started to travel down her body gently ... feeling every inch of her, her breathing stayed calm.

Hanjun didn't speak for several minutes. He took the time to not pressure her in any way. Resting his hands back on her waist, he kissed her forehead softly, still with closed eyes.

He took every second he had to touch her whole body, not leaving a single part out. Assured that every part had the same attention as the other, he was satisfied with his work.

Bending down, he found her lips and kissed her gently.

"Open them," she whispered against his chest.

Slowly opening them, he didn't even look at her body first. The first thing he looked at were her eyes. The eyes, he fell in love with.

***

"How are you sweetheart?"

"A bit sleepy but fine, don't worry."

"What do you wanna do?"

"Sunset," Yoon-Rae and Ae-Cha said at the same time.

"I love you," Yoon-Rae whispered, kissing her neck softly. Ae-Cha took his hand and put it on her belly. "They'll have the best father on Earth."

Kissing her hand, he got lost in her eyes even after years of marriage. "And their mother will always be remembered, I'll make sure of that."

***

"Jade, are you ready for your new choreographer?"

"A new one? I thought we would stay with the one we have."

"Well, she will stay at our company but now you'll have a personal choreographer just for you."

"She was my personal choreographer, Junghoon."

"You know what I mean. Let's go. He's waiting in the practice room."

"He? I've only had women before for a reason, Junghoon."

"Yes, yes but he's great. Trust me."

"He's in there. I have to go now. Just learn a little bit of the new choreography, and then finish the work in the studio. You know, it's for the award show that will be held soon."

"You mean the award show in which I will dance with Hanjun?"

"Yes, that one. Today, you'll learn the spicy choreography I told you about. If you have any problem, call me and we will review it. Hanjun will come later to train with you and the choreographer."

"Aunty, who this person?" Dae-Jung asked. He was already inside of the room, and Jade chased after him. She kneeled to him and while she glanced up, a green eye pair met hers.

Jade's eyes went down his body. He had quite broad shoulders and a sharp jaw line. His tall upper body looked good, and you could see through his white shirt that he had massive abs, though not as much as Hanjun, but you could see them perfectly without him tense them.

"Hello, I'm Brian. Nice to meet you, Jade."

"Jade, Junghoon said you're here so—" Hanjun looked up and saw Brian next to Jade.

"Hanjun, come and meet my new choreographer. His name is Brian. He will teach us our choreography for the award show."

"Well, nice to meet you, Hanjun."

"Hello, Brian," he turned around and faced Jade.

He stared at Jade and spoke silently to her. "A man?" his lips formed. Jade shrugged her shoulders and faced Brian. "Let's repeat everything from the start."

It didn't take them long to learn the whole choreography. In just eight days, both had the whole choreography down. Even Brian was impressed by them. He clapped at the corner as the music stopped.

"Well done, you two. It looks good for the short time we trained, but there is still much air up. The award show is in September. So, no worries about it."

***

Jade's eyebrow raised. "Hanjun, we're training."

He looked down to her, his hands wrapping around her taille, pulling her closer to him. "I don't care, Love," he whispered in her ears with lust. Jade licked her lips and stared at him again.

"Fuck," his voice was breathless as he stared at her lips.

"Stop staring at my lips and kiss me."

He sighed, "If I kiss you, I'm not sure I'll be able to stop."

Jade smiled, "Then don't stop."

His eyes shut and he took a deep breath.

With that specific sentence Jade allows him to feel free and fuck her for the very first time.

"I want our first time to be good, not only at the couch in the practice room."

"I don't care, Hanjun."

"I will have a limit today but next time, there won't be a limit. Be ready for it," his eyes opened, and he grabbed her face smashing his lips onto hers. Sliding down her sides, his hands traveled further while his tongue dominated.

One hand placed at her side, the other on her lower back bringing them closer to one another.

Their bodies had no space between them as the kiss continued. Leaving Jade breathlessly, his hand reached to the back of her thighs, tugging her up a bit. You could only hear their strong breathing and the sound of bodies against each other. Nothing else. Wrapping her thighs around his waist, his hands placed themselves on them. Gripping onto his shirt, her hands slid up his chest to his shoulders leaving wet kisses on his neck.

Starting to play with the band of her black leggings, Jade let out a small chuckle, "Closed door?" speaking against his lips returning to the kiss.

"Hm."

Colliding with the soft couch in the room, her hands traveled down his body.

Hanjun pushed his body on hers, keeping her on the couch.

She had no chance to win against him. Trapped in his grip, she let out soft moans as soon as Hanjun was nipping onto her sweet spot.

Grabbing his face, he used both hands to take her wrists and placed them above her head. His lips leaving red spots on her neck and jaw, trailing down to her collar bones and stopping at the strap of Jade's sports bra.

Trailing back up, his lips met hers. She wrapped her legs around him tighter while he placed his hands on her waist, walking to the glass door of the practice room.

One hand under Jade's ass, he drew the curtains to the door. Placing both of his hands on her waist, he brought her back to the couch. Sitting on it, she straddled his lap, tucking onto his hair, lead him to groan. The kiss was still aggressive and fast. But still, respectful and full of love.

Kissing down his neck, her hands traveled lower on his body. They reached his sweatpants but suddenly, Hanjun stopped her. His big hands touched her tiny one before she could do anything.

"Not here, Love. As much as I want it, not here."

"But—"

He shook his head, leading Jade to feel insecure. She said, "I'm sorry."

"What? No, don't be sorry. It's okay, really. It's just not the best place for it, my Love."

Lifting her chin with his finger, he kissed her nose gently, "Okay?"

"Hm."

"Words, Love. I need words."

"Yes, it's okay."

Placing several pecks on her face, he lifted her from his lap to stand on the floor. "Did I ruin the atmosphere?"

"A bit, but it's okay," replying to him, she kissed him gently.

"There will be other days, better days. Trust me."

Hugging her tightly, his hands stayed on her waist pulling away. "Another round? Gosh, you're driving me crazy. How can you not be tired yet?"

"Well, I'm a real gentleman who knows how to take care of a lady."

Hanjun pulled Jade by her hand into the middle of the room before letting her hand go and walking to the door. Opening the curtains and turning the music on, he walked back with a smile.

Hanjun stretched his hand out, Jade took it and got pulled in his arms. He kissed her neck softly before he started to dance. Getting a lot of attention, several trainees surrounded the big glass door to watch their training.

"Last round," he mumbled to Jade.
His hands crossed above his head while he stared to the floor, his left foot was in front of the right foot, also crossed.
She had her hands around his neck, and her head was slightly turned to face the mirror while one of her legs was around his torso. Their faces were inches apart, the music stopped.
Hanjun pulled away and clapped quietly.
Putting her hands on her knees, she bent over to catch her breath. Hanjun sat on the floor closing his eyes.
Standing up, they hugged each other briefly until Jade pulled away, realizing they had an audience. Walking away, Jade was covering herself with her jacket, taking her bag and waited at the glass door for him.
The trainees in front of the door took a few steps away for them to pass.

\*\*\*

Closing the studio, she put her shoes back on and walked tiredly with the flashlight of her phone, during the company. The clock on the wall was flashing through the whole cafeteria. It read 2 a.m. It was already past 3 a.m. when she got home. Jade took a shower, changed into her pajamas, and rushed in the bed. Hanjun was sleeping in the middle of the bed, but only half of his body was under the blanket. Squishing herself next to his big chest, she pulled the whole blanket over them. Drifting off to sleep in his arms, she let her hands stay around his neck, hoping he would have left before the morning's actually here. As much as Jade wishes to wake up next to him, he has to leave.
They can't be seen by the boys. They just can't risk it. He has to leave before anyone is awake.

Jade woke up again, **alone**. Of course, it's better like that.
The bed is huge without Hanjun next to her, and, to be honest without him, it looks kinda scary being on it.
Walking downstairs, she found her phone charging near the fridge. Picking it up, she saw a message from Hanjun.
*I hope I'll see you at the music video scene for B'ONE's next comeback.* <3

He was alone in the room when Jade joined him. "Hi."
Jade walked over to him and kissed him softly on the cheek. He turned around and faced her completely. Hugging her tightly, he put his chin on top of her head. Still in Hanjun's arms, she placed her hands on his chest.
"Another one," he said, pouting. "But here," and he pointed with his index finger at his lips.
Smiling, she stood on her tiptoes and tried reaching him. Chuckling about the height difference, he bent down. Kissing her, he walked backward to the chair next to the table and pulled her down on his lap. She made herself comfortable and tried without many movements to get to it.
"Stop doing this, Love," he said with a deep voice.
"I didn't want—" Jade tried to reply but got cut off by his lips. He pulled away, smiling at her. Jade leaned to his face, their foreheads touching. One of her hands gently brushing his hair while the other stayed on the cheek. "We have to be more careful, Hanjun," Jade whispered, her hands running through his hair, their foreheads still touching.
"What do you mean, Love?"
"You know what I mean. The last few weeks? How we weren't that careful? The incident?"
"You mean with the candy? Oh, c'mon, I told them I just tried yours."
"And you think they believe that?"
Jade was talking about an incident which happened and almost ruined their secret.
All the members were in the café downstairs in the building as Hanjun got there, too. Walking toward them, Alex asked why

his tongue was purple, and he simply replied that he had just eaten a blue lollipop.

The boys looked at him confused, when Jade walked through the door, heading straight to the toilet with a red lollipop.

"OH MY GOSH!" "WHAT THE HELL?!" "NO WAY!" "AHHHH!!" were the various expressions given from the boys.

Hanjun's eyes widen for a moment before he turned to the boys and convinced them, after speaking for about half an hour, that he just tried Jade's lollipop because he wasn't sure if he would like the flavor or not.

Hanjun lifted her chin up, pecking her lips again. "I'll try to be more careful, Darling."

"It's not that I don't want to tell them. I'm just scared they won't—" she got cut off by another kiss.

"It's okay, Love."

Kai and Sanghoon stood behind the camera, watching the others shooting a special scene.

"Where's Hanjun? We need him in a few seconds, too," a staff member said.

"We will look for him," Kai said, pulling Sanghoon with him.

They opened a few rooms' doors, but he wasn't in any of them. There was one last room; he had to be in there.

Sanghoon spoke with Kai while opening the door, his back was faced with Jade onto Hanjun's lap.

While Sanghoon couldn't see a thing, Kai saw everything, staring at them.

Confusing Sanghoon with it, he also turned around. He froze in his position, also staring at them.

Jade immediately got off Hanjun's lap. Hanjun stood up, straightening his trousers.

"What the hell just happened?" Sanghoon asked, looking from Hanjun to Jade.

Jade glanced at Hanjun, he nodded. Neither of them wanted to lie to them, so they told them about their dating.

There was a long silent minute before Kai turned his head to Sanghoon. "You owe me 20,"

Sanghoon sighed out loud and took his phone out.

"I won. I get 20. I get 20. You owe me 20," Kai repeated over and over.

"I sent it to you, right now. Got it?"

"Yes, thank you," Kai replied with a huge smile.

"You bet on us?"

"Well, kinda," Kai put his phone in his pocket.

"Let's go get the others. I wanna get my money."

"Shut up," Sanghoon added, while hitting him on his chest.

"Why do you need us?" Joonwoo asked, standing in the door-frame, behind him were all the other members.

"Jade and Hanjun are dating," Kai said, but immediately put his hand over his mouth.

"I'm sorry," he turned around to Jade and Hanjun.

Hanjun gripped Jade's hand tightly. "It's okay."

Kai turned back to the others. "In that case, you all owe me 20." The members stared for a few seconds at them before pulling their phone out to send the money to Kai.

"Dinner tonight? It's on me," he added, laughing.

"Sure, why not?"

"Where?"

"Let's discuss this later. Hanjun, you have your shoot now," Joonwoo added.

Hanjun kissed Jade on the forehead before all of them followed Joonwoo to the set.

Jade was honestly very glad the boys didn't point it out or asked stupid questions right after they found it out. They acted as if it's normal, a normal relationship between two lovers. Can you call it lovers? Or are they just more than friends but less than lovers?

*** 

"Yoon-Rae, don't worry about me. Enjoy your time with your wife. It's okay. There will be plenty of chances for us to see each other."

"But—"

"If you don't agree, I'm gonna hang up this phone and won't call you ever again. Take your wife out or something. I know we are best friends, but that doesn't mean we have to hang out every second in our life."

"It's only been a week, gosh. We can drink a coffee tomorrow at work," hanging up the phone, she sighed out loud.

Yoon-Rae and Jade didn't meet up for a bit longer than a week because Yoon-Rae was stressed about the birth, and Jade didn't want to give them less time to be together.

He feels so bad about it, but Jade won't give in. He needs to spend the last few days with his wife, Ae-Cha. Not his best friend, and that's why they didn't talk that much in the last few days.

When he came to work, either Jade or he was busy. Afterward, she didn't want to bother them.

***

"Jade, it is so nice to see you. Thank you so much for looking after Dae-Jung."

"I hope you still got some time before you leave."

"I have a whole day with him today, all thanks to you."

"I'll visit you in the hospital with him, don't worry."

Ae-Cha smiled at her and took Dae-Jung in her arms. "Let's have a great day together, huh?"

"Yes, Mummy."

"All right, goodbye, Ae-Cha."

"Goodbye, Jade," she said smiling, hugging Jade tightly. "Thank you for everything."

"I love you, Ae-Cha. You're one of the best and strongest women I've ever met."

"Look good to them."

"I will," hugging her again, a tear escaped Jade's eyes.

"Hey, it's okay. You'll be okay."

Just nodding, Ae-Cha hugged her again.

***

The days passed, and it was already the day of the birth.
Jade was with Dae-Jung at her house while Yoon-Rae and Ae-Cha were in the labor room.
She said her goodbye while crying; Jade cannot imagine how hard it's gonna be for Yoon- Rae.
Jade hasn't known Ae-Cha for long. Yoon-Rae married her many years ago. He will be destroyed.
Jade has to be ready. It won't be easy.
Especially not with the hate Yoon-Rae has been experiencing recently. Yoon-Rae just lived his life, and toxic fans suddenly started rumors about him, hating on him and more stuff. It got so bad, the company had to post an article about it.
It's not right to do that. If you just don't like an idol, don't waste your time hating on them. They did nothing wrong. Some even accused him of hitting his members.

Yoon-Rae was with Ae-Cha in the labor.
She would soon give birth.
Yoon-Rae was standing next to her, already crying about the fact both could die.
It still wasn't sure. But she won't live, that's for sure.
The kid does have a quite high chance to live, the mother unfortunately not.
"You can do it. I believe in you. I love you," he whispered and kissed Ae-Cha's wet forehead.
After seven hours and a bit more pushing, the doctor turned to a nurse.
**"Time of birth 8:34."**
Handing Yoon-Rae and Ae-Cha their newborn daughter, Yoon-Rae brushed Ae-Cha's hair out of her face.
"Look at her. She is totally like you, Yoon-Rae."
"But she has your eyes, Sweetheart."
"I love you."
"I love you, Ae-Cha, forever and always. Thank you for the amazing time I could spend with you," and then he kissed her for the last time.

**"Time of death, 8:47."**
Closing the eyes of Ae-Cha, he looked up at Yoon-Rae, "I wish you only the best, Mr. Seo."
Yoon-Rae looked down at her with tears in his eyes.
"Miss? he spoke up."
"Yes, Mr. Seo?"
"Could you take her for a second?"
"Of course," she took his newborn in her arms while Yoon-Rae sat down.
"Can I help with anything, or would you like to have a few minutes alone with her?"
"Could you call the person with the name Jade Evans, please, and tell her—" his voice broke.
"I'll tell her," the nurse said with a soft smile.

Jade walked with Dae-Jung's hand in hers into the hospital.
"Miss Evans?" a nurse said.
"Yes?" Jade turned around and faced a nurse younger than her.
"Follow me."
Jade nodded and walked with Dae-Jung next to the nurse.
"He's in this room."
"Dae-Jung, could you stay with this woman for a second?"
Nodding, Jade looked at the nurse, and she nodded as well.
Opening the door, she saw Yoon-Rae sitting next to the bed where Ae-Cha still laid on. He didn't even look up. He just stared at her dead body.
Walking slowly toward him, she laid her hand on his shoulder.
"I'm here for you, and if you need anything just say it."
"How is Daddy?" Dae-Jung asked, worried.
"He will get better."
"Can I see him?"
Jade didn't answer and just opened the door.
"Daddy?" Dae-Jung asked quietly.
Looking up, he saw his little boy standing next to the door with tears in his eyes.
"Hey, little boy."

"Do you think Mummy will like it up there?"

"I hope so," he answered softly.

Dae-Jung crawled onto Yoon-Rae's lap and cuddled against his big chest.

"Will you miss her?"

"I've been missing her the moment she left."

"I didn't want Mummy to leave."

"Me neither, Bear. Me neither."

Yoon-Rae gave him a little kiss on the back of his head.

Pressing his lips together, he tried to hold his tears in.

He doesn't want to cry—

—not in front of Dae-Jung.

\*\*\*

A stable newborn and two broken men could finally go back home. Without the laugh of Ae-Cha, without her voice speaking, her cooking or her music, the house was so empty.

"I'll come back later to watch the kids, all right?" Jade said, while hugging Yoon-Rae.

Without saying a word, he nodded, closing the door.

Dae-Jung took his hand and walked with him to the little bed in which Jin-Ae was lying.

"She has Mummy's eyes."

"She has," Yoon-Rae tried to smile. "You're already so smart at this age, just like Mummy."

"Just like Mummy," Dae-Jung repeated what his dad said.

\*\*\*

Since the birth of Jin-Ae and the loss of Ae-Cha, Yoon-Rae was going through a really bad time. Everything reminded him of her. On top of that, the hate didn't stop. It got even worse. He got death threats, more accusations, and bad rumors.

Slowly, he started to believe what the people on the internet told him. How bad he is. That no one wants him alive. He should just kill himself. Giving the world some pleasure by killing himself, by leaving the group, stopping with his music.

—cause no one wants to listen to his shit anyway. And the worst thing is— he didn't talk to anyone about it. He didn't want to bother them with his problems. Not his members, or even Jade. It was too much for him, and he gave his kids for two days to Sanghoon and his girlfriend.

The thing is, Yoon-Rae didn't attend to work on the first day, and he never missed work. Something's odd, and Sanghoon doesn't know what.

Walking with Dae-Jung into Jade's studio, he looked concerned. Dae-Jung's sister was with Lia at home because neither the boys nor the company knows about Yoon-Rae's second child yet.

Running to Jade as soon as he saw her. Dae-Jung hugged her tightly. Asking him where his dad is, Sanghoon just looked at her. He didn't look happy, he looked more worried.

"Jade, we need to talk. Now."

Dae-Jung took Jade's hand in his to play while she talked with Sanghoon.

"Is something wrong?"

"Yoon-Rae didn't attend work."

"He's probably just late, don't worry."

"Jade, he's never late. Can you drive up to his house and check in on him? For me? Please?"

"I'll go right now."

Pulling the car harshly over, she shut her door.

What if something bad happened? Was she too late? Could she help him?

She ran to the door of his house and knocked several times.

"Yoon-Rae? Yoon-Rae are you there?" she sighed and searched in her bag for the keys.

Finding them, she opened the door after several tries. Jade ran to the living room, bathroom, and kitchen, where she saw a knife was missing. She got scared and ran upstairs. The door to his bedroom was closed.

Opening it, she ran into the room, where she saw him. He stood in the middle of the room, holding a knife and some blood streamed down his wrist.

"Yoon-Rae ..." she couldn't speak further.

Jade walked slowly toward him.

"Don't come near me!" he screamed. "Please, just don't come near me!" his voice broke.

"Yoon-Rae, let me help you. Please, you have a family. Your kids need you. They can't lose their father right after their mother died."

Silence filled the room. Staring at each other, his grip around the knife loosens.

"I just didn't think it would be that hard. Everything reminds me of her. Everything, I can't even look into the eyes of my own daughter. It is horrible," his voice raised a bit.

And even though Jade is scared, she shut her feelings away. Now is not the time for her problems. He needs her.

After talking with him, Jade walked slowly toward him, catching the knife in his hand, and throwing it next to the door. Instantly, she hugged Yoon-Rae very tight. "I'm here. Let everything out."

Staying like this for a moment, Yoon-Rae let go. He glanced at her with teary eyes.

"You should be at work," he whispered.

"Same goes for you," she whispered back.

"I think it is time to tell them."

Yoon-Rae nodded, and Jade walked out of the room to get some bandages. She had to look for them really hard before she found them.

Coming back, she saw Yoon-Rae sitting on the bed; in his hand was the knife and tears in his eyes.

"Yoon-Rae—" her voice broke. Jade ran to him and looked with tears in her eyes in his.

One time being caught hurting themselves is definitely something different than being caught two times in less than an hour. He needs comfort and help, and Jade is there to give him that.

She hugged him tightly and whispered: "You and your kids will live with me for a while."

She didn't ask for permission, if he's okay with it; she just decided how it will be.

"I'll write Sanghoon, so he'll bring them after today to me."

"Jade?" he asked with tears in his eyes.

"Yes, Yoon-Rae?"

"Could you not tell Sanghoon about this incident, please?"

"I won't tell him, but we will tell Dowoon."

Yoon-Rae was sitting next to Jade while she's packing his children's stuff. His whole body was still shaking a bit. Yoon-Rae's stuff was already packed.

Jade ran her hand through her hair and took some long breaths before she goes on.

"Can I help you?" he asked concerned.

"Arrange a meeting with Dowoon as soon as possible. The best would be today," she answered softly.

"Hello, Yoon-Rae. Do you feel better, or are you still sick?" Dowoon asked on the phone.

Yoon-Rae couldn't speak and stared at his feet.

"Yoon-Rae, are you there? ...Yoon-Rae?"

Standing up, Jade took the phone out of his hand.

"Hello, Dowoon. It's Jade."

"Jade? Why are you with Yoon-Rae. Isn't he sick?"

"Do you have time for a meet?"

"Is there a problem I should know?"

"Well, yes. There is. Can we meet?"

"Who?"

"Yoon-Rae, you and me."

"Sure, I have time now if that's good for you."

"We'll be there in half an hour," she glanced at Yoon-Rae, who still stared at his feet.

"See you," he said before hanging up the phone. Jade went to Yoon-Rae and pulled him up gently.

"Everything will be okay," she whispered and hugged him softly.

"Hello, together. Come in," Dowoon said.

"Hello," both replied quietly.

Jade pushed Yoon-Rae a little and walked next to him to their seats.

"It's nice to see you two together. What did you want to talk about? Will there be a collaboration between you or—"

"No, and unfortunately, it is not a very nice meet today."

"What happened?" he asked, confused.

After taking some deep breaths, Yoon-Rae looked up. "My wife, she—," his voice broke, and he started to cry.

Dowoon didn't understand anything and looked at Jade, perplexed. Jade laid her hand on Yoon-Rae's arm and started to explain.


"Wow, Yoon-Rae, I don't know how to put this in words—"

"I'm really sorry for this loss."

"Well, actually there's more."

"More?"

Jade nodded and looked at Yoon-Rae.

# CHAPTER 6

Yoon-Rae didn't say anything and pulled up the sleeves of his hoodie. Around his wrist were bandages, and you didn't need to see the blood to tell what happened.

"Yoon-Rae, I can't believe you—"

"He did, and it is not okay. I want him to go to a psychiatrist."

"Of course, we will search for one as soon as possible."

"As soon as possible?"

"Are you joking right now, Dowoon?"

"I can't believe you. He is **in pain**; he hurt himself."

"He lost his wife and has to raise two children on his own, as if this wouldn't be enough, the shoot of their comeback is so important so he can't have a break?!" she asked unbelievably.

"The hate keeps going on, and nothing happened after this shitty article the company posted. What's wrong with you?"

"Jade, I know, you think this is really bad but trust me, we'll search for one, and he can get treated as soon as possible. It isn't so bad, you know."

"It isn't so bad? It isn't so fucking bad?"

"The only thing in your head is how you can make good money," Jade almost yelled.

"I know, what you mean, and I know what this feels li—"

"No, you know nothing about this. You didn't hurt yourself just because you thought you're not good enough, because you lost someone, because you didn't think you'll make it until tomorrow, because you have depression, and you wanted to stop all of this. You didn't try to kill yourself but failed. After you failed, you didn't have to act like nothing happened, and this **several times**."

"No, you didn't. Because all you do is sit behind this fucking desk and make money. I won't let you make him suffer the way I did. I don't want anyone to suffer like I did. I won't let him try to kill himself and if he fails, to act like nothing happened. No one deserves this, so please let him—" her voice broke.

"Jade, I didn't know you—"

"Jade—" Yoon-Rae said in shock and pulled her in.

"I have to tell this Junghoon, you know this, right?"

"He already knows it," she said quietly.

"Are you in therapy?"

Jade nodded slightly.

"Do you think this psychiatrist would have a place for Yoon-Rae?"

"I'll ask Junghoon."

***

Hanjun was heading to Jade's house.

All the boys were also there to eat lunch, and then spend their weekend off together. They decided to go to Jade because it is closer to the town than their mansion.

He was late, **very late**.

Hanjun canceled many of their dates over the last two weeks, and he was also very suspicious. He wasn't home at the time he should've been. He didn't text her much. Didn't call her nor spoke to her in the company. And arguing about moving in together was one of their latest hobbies together.

The last fight was three days ago.

It was also the day they saw each other last.

Jade tells him every time, she isn't ready for this yet and was scared about the fans, too.

It was three weeks after the death of Ae-Cha. Yoon-Rae is still feeling extremely bad, and Jade tries helping him as much as possible. Two weeks ago, Yoon-Rae hurt himself but luckily, Jade found him on time. Now, Yoon-Rae and his two kids were living with Jade. Dae-Jung was with the boys in the living room when Hanjun came in, while Jin-Ae slept in a room upstairs.

He didn't even let Jade say hello. He just pulled her by her wrist to the part of the kitchen that was separate with a door to the rest of the kitchen.

"Honey, is everything all right?"

"Everything all right? What do you think—"

"You didn't think I would find it out, did you? The real reason why you don't want to move in with me."

"Honey, I've told you the reason—"

"You've told me lies. Lies, nothing more."

"Wha—"

"When did you plan to tell me? You and Yoon-Rae? Living together? What is the meaning of this? You live with him but not with me?"

"Hanjun, you've misunderstood something, please—"

"Misunderstood? What could I have misunderstood? Jade, he has a fucking **wife** and a **kid**. Why are you living with him?"

Jade flinched at his tone, taking one step back. It was the first time Hanjun yelled at her in this tone. Of course, they've argued before but never in this tone.

While Jade took another step back, he moved one step forward.

"Hanjun, please—"

**"Did you fuck him already?"**

"Wha-"

"You know what? I guess this is why your father and your sister hate you. Why your mother left you alone with your father. All because you can't have just one thing, you need **everything**," Hanjun yelled.

"What—"

"Yes, you heard right. Your own father doesn't even love you. What family is like this? Only a **broken one**."

"Hanjun, this is enough!" Yoon-Rae stepped in between them, taking Jade in his arms.

"Get the hell out Yoon-Rae.", he yelled at him.

"Who do you think you're talking to?" he said calmly back.

"You've fucked the wrong woman, Yoon-Rae. You have a wife and a kid. Why would you live with Jade?"

"I'll leave," Jade mumbled, running to her door, picking her keys up and shutting the door behind her.

Yoon-Rae wanted to chase her after, but he got held by Hanjun. "Don't you dare to run after her," he said angrily. "We aren't done yet."

"What the fuck is wrong with you? You yelled at your girlfriend who has depression and anxiety."

"And, what the hell is wrong with you? You've fucked my girlfriend even though you have a wife and a kid."

"I have two kids, and my wife is dead, Hanjun. Don't think you know everything because you know nothing at all. Jade was the one who looked after me. She kept me away from killing myself on that day. I've lost my wife, and I've had only Jade, and now I'm not even sure if I still have her," he yelled at him in frustration.

At this time, the boys and Dae-Jung were standing in the door, all of them heard the yelling. Sanghoon lifted Dae-Jung up, hugging him tightly, while walking away with him.

Hanjun stared at him in disbelief. "Yoon-Rae—"

"I have to find Jade before anything bad happens," Yoon-Rae said out of breath, leaving the boys alone in Jade's house.

Hanjun's hand started shaking as he tried to control his breath. Jae noticed it and ran over to him. "Hey, look at me."

"I yelled at her, Hyung."

"I scared her, Hyung."

"I broke her trust, Hyung."

Struggling to actually catch his breath, Jae held his hands. "Hanjun, look at me. Breathe with me, okay?"

"Hyung, I—"

"I can't—, can't breathe."

"You can. Look at me."

And finally looking up, Jae didn't break their eye contact. "Good, now breathe."

Hanjun can't have a panic attack right now. Jade wasn't here anymore, and the members all struggle a bit to calm him down since he had this one big panic attack. And since Jade got here, she did it all the time, having no problem with it.

But the members? They still struggle, even after Jade told them what to do. They need time for it, and they cannot be stressed or else it won't work.

But time? They don't have time right now.

Catching his own breathing after some time, he stared at the floor before taking his key, running out of the mansion.

"Hanjun, wait—"

Too late. He's already gone.

'I yelled at her and thought she cheated.'

'I'm a bad person. I promised her, to never hurt her.'

'I broke my promise.'

'She will never forgive me.'

'Jade was only helping Yoon-Rae get over the death of his wife,' Hanjun kept repeating in his head.

Trying not to have another panic attack, he took a deep breath pressing the gas looking for Jade.


"C'mon, Jade. Pick up," Si-woo said. He was walking through the living room, and next to him, Eric tries calling Yoon-Rae. It has been two days since Jade was missing.

Looking up, Si-woo shook his head for a no but then—

Eric glanced at him, and Si-woo tried to explain that Jade picked up. Si-woo put her on speaker without saying it. "Jade?"

"Si-woo, why— are you ... calling?"

"Oh my God, Jade. I was so worried about you. Are you okay? Where are you?"

"I'm ... on a cliff."

"You're on a cliff?" Si-woo gasped.

Jade's voice was very thin and anxious.

"Jade?"

"On which cliff are you?" he asked calmly.

"I ... I'm—, I'm on the—", but the connection suddenly broke down. Si-woo tried calling her again and again but nothing happened.


"Where could she be?" Yoon-Rae said to himself while driving around the town. He didn't stop once for a break. He has been in the car for two days straight.

He stopped at the red traffic light when he got a call from Eric.

"Eric?"

"Yes, it's me. Jade is on a cliff, but we don't know on which."

"Are you driving right now?"

"You're on speaker, don't worry."

"We have to be fast. Si-woo is still trying to call her, but we don't know for how long she could actually answer."

"Where could she be?" Joonwoo asked nervously.

"We'll find her, don't worry too much," Kai said.

"And Hanjun is still out there. If he has another panic attack—"

"Joonwoo, everything will go well."

"But—"

"Hyung, look at me."

Holding his hands, Kai did some small breathing exercises with Joonwoo.

"Everything will be alright."

The group has separated themselves a day ago so they could find her easily but with no success yet.

Sanghoon stayed at home with Dae-Jung and his sister.

'If Jade's gonna take her life, it would be my fault.'

'No, please. I can't live without her,' Hanjun thought, breathing heavily. He ran his hand through his hair and pulled his car into a parking lot. 'Where could she be?'

"Hanjun?"

"Yoon-Rae, look, I'm—"

"I don't want to hear anything from you, all right?! I wanted to ask about Jade. I don't care about you at the moment."

"I understand that."

"Do you have any ideas where she could be?"

"There's nothing in my head," he whispered.

"Jade told Si-woo, she's on a cliff. Is there a cliff she likes?"

"Daepo Jusangjeolli Cliff."

"What?"

"Daepo Jusangjeolli Cliff," Hanjun repeated himself. "It is the cliff we like the most."

"I'm like ten or even more away. This is too long. Where are you?"

"I'll be there in less than two. Let the members know that I'm driving there now."

"If you do anything wrong, I'll kill you."

"I know what I did wrong. Trust me," Hanjun said before hanging up.

Two steps and finally everything would come to an end. There are only two steps to take.

Her whole life, trying to end it. This would be her final chance. It wouldn't disappoint anyone; her mother doesn't care about her and so doesn't her brother, and let's not bring her father and sister in this.

The boys? They are probably very glad if she wouldn't be here anymore.

And Hanjun? Hanjun, the man she loves but is too scared to tell him? Maybe she would regret not telling him but right now, he doesn't want her anyway. He thinks she's a loser and a cheater. He doesn't love her at all.

He wouldn't be sad if she won't be here anymore.

Just one last step, and it would be done. Done forever.

**One step**, which would change so many lives.

But why is it so hard? She has nothing, right? Or does she have something? Is she finally appreciated? Is she finally loved? It couldn't be, right? Who wants a broken person if they can have several happy and healthy persons?

Closing the eyes, she took a deep breath.

"It's time," Jade mumbled. "It's the right thing," she tried convincing herself.

# CHAPTER 7

"Jade!" someone screamed with tears in their eyes. Jade flinched at the voice.

Is it really him? Is it possible?

"Jade, please. Turn around," he almost whispered.

Turning around, there he was. Hanjun, the person she loves the most.

Without saying the words, she feels it. There were so many perfect times, she could have said it, but every time she tried, the words got stuck in her throat. And Hanjun? He never told Jade how much he loved her. He is scared. Scared, she wouldn't accept him, or she would leave him. Do they not see what everyone else sees?

Like, why? C'mon. Just say it. It's only three words. Eight letters and one sentence. It's not that hard.

But why would the person who just yelled at her a few days ago currently be here? Why does he seem to care?

Hanjun was running toward her and hugged Jade tightly. "Don't go," he whispered.

Jade stood still before she pulled him tighter to her laying her head on his chest.

"Don't leave me."

"I'm sorry, Jade. I'm so sorry, Jade. Please ... Please, just don't go," he whispered again.

Jade slowly lifted her head, seeing into Hanjun's teary eyes. Removing one of her hands, she wiped a tear off.

"Jade, can you ever forgive me?"

"Hanjun, I—"

"I've had three such hard weeks, and then I was very jealous about you and Yoon-Rae having such a strong connection to each other and—"

"Hanjun," she said softly again.

"I know, this isn't an excuse for what I did but—", he looked at her with tears in his eyes. "I love you," he whispered. "I really do."
Is this a dream? Did he really just—
Wow. He really said it.
It was right for Jade to hesitate. To wait and to fail every single suicide attempt. Someone on this Earth does love her. But does he really mean it? What if he just said it without meaning it?
"Why do you love me? What is the special thing about me?" not comprehending why; it was the only thing she could ask. "I'm broken. I'm diagnosed with depression and anxiety. There are women out there who are perfect. Unlike me," she spoke in disbelief.
"Jade, I love you because of **you**. I'll always love you no matter what will happen in the future ..."
"**I** wanna be the person helping you get over everything."
"**I** wanna be the person you feel the most comfortable with."
"**I** wanna be the person you'll wake up next to every morning."
"**I** wanna love you the way you've never been loved."
"**I** wanna stay with you until I die."
"But how can you love **me**? That's not true. I do not deserve this."
"You do deserve this! You suffered enough, and it's time for you to be loved."
Jade had tears in her eyes, still not believing it.
"My Love, look at me. Some things just are and always will be that way. I love you by heart, and even if you don't believe it, I still lose myself every time I look into your eyes ... I love you, Jade Evans."
A smile appeared on Jade's lips. Her eyes got teary; she closed them slowly.
Hanjun finally did it. He told her his feelings. He's never done that before. It was the first time Hanjun has found a girl he loves. Every girl wanted him for fame, for money but Jade— For the first time in his life, he was sure, she was different.
Bending down, Hanjun felt Jade's soft lips against his own. The kiss was tender, feeling each other's lips softly on their own. Both telling, they love each other without saying it.

And as much as Hanjun wants to hear the words from Jade, he will wait for her because she is someone he doesn't want to lose.

"Mr. Kim and Mrs. Evans-Kim, we would appreciate if we could go home now."

"Don't you guys know what privacy means?" Hanjun said, laughing as Jade hid her face in his chest.

Getting home, Sanghoon was with both kids on the couch. While the members joined them watching the movie, Jade and Hanjun went upstairs to their room.

Hanjun closed the bedroom door quietly behind them and smiled at Jade. A smile she knows too well.

"Honey, they are downstairs. Not now."

He came slowly to her and hugged her tightly while whispering in her ear, "Darling, let me show you how much you mean to me. Let me give you what you deserve. Let me take care of you—"

"No, not now."

Kissing her briefly, he walked out of the room.

Closing the door with a smile, knowing, Yoon-Rae sleeps happily with his kids behind this door, she walked away. The boys were all downstairs sleeping together under the blanket Jade put over them.

Jade went to her shared room with Hanjun where he was already in the big bathroom when Jade walked in. Feeling his burning gaze on her, she tried not to blush. And still, as she walked past him to the shower, his gaze never left her for a single moment.

Turning it on, the hot water was running down her body. She sighed and put the water on the hottest when suddenly a hand rushed past her and turned the heat down.

"Too hot isn't good for you, Darling," Hanjun said with a deep voice and brushed a hair behind her ear.

"Get the hell out," she said, laughing.

"And what if I don't want to?"

"Move, I don't care about you right now."

"Don't lie to me."

Jade didn't look down at him, she stared right into his eyes, "The boys are over. I'm not fucking you. They'll hear it."

"I'm not fucking you tonight. I'll show you my love for you tonight," he said, with a smirk before he left the shower.

Jade finally got out of the shower. She put on only a loose shirt without any underwear.

Getting out of the bathroom, she saw Hanjun laying on the bed, with a shirt which wasn't buttoned up and his jogger pants low on his hips.

Jade tried to move through the room as she felt her nipples getting hard. She already felt turned on, and Hanjun didn't do anything more than stare at her.

"Is something bothering you, Darling?" he suddenly asked with his deep voice and made Jade shiver.

Sometimes, Jade thinks, he likes using his deep voice to make her all his … because he knows what his voice does to her.

"Hmm, no, nothing is bothering me," she said after putting her dirty clothes in the laundry basket, and, as Jade did that, she saw him looking at her even more intensely. Jade blushed because she knew what was on his mind.

"Cuddle?" he asked suddenly with a cute and soft voice. Definitely not what Jade thought he was thinking, but she smiled anyway and went over to him.

Jade hugged him tightly as he put his head on her boobs. Hanjun gave her a peck on her lips and started moving around. Still giving her pecks all over her face while being on top of her, leaving Jade's thought somewhere else.

"I thought we would only cuddle," she said, chuckling. "C'mon, let's go to sleep. You'll wake the others."

"Later. We can go to sleep later," he said, mumbling. Giving her a peck on her forehead, he started trailing down her neck.

He stared in her eyes. Her brown eyes, in which the lights reflected and let some sparkles in her iris. Bending down again, he started kissing her lips passionately a few times, not giving her time to actually breathe.

Jade turned her face and kissed him on his cheek.

"Stay still, Jade," he whispered, kissing her neck while coming further up with his whole body.

Jade let him do it, and she started to undress him.

He gave her a few more pecks and looked down at her smiling. The smile is back, hell yeah.

Sucking on her neck, she replied with a soft moan.

His hands traveled near her waist, pulling the shirt further up.

Arching her back, her hips moved closer against his. Her lips separated, filling the room with soft moans.

"Hanjun, don't stop," she said, breathing heavily. Her hands gripped in his hair, tugging on it while pressing her head into the pillow.

"I told you, too hot isn't good for you," whispering against her lips, a smirk on his.

Only now did Jade understand what he meant in the shower. It had a double meaning, of course. The flirty Hanjun is back.

Pushing himself away from her, he looked in her disappointed and frustrated face.

Not giving her time to process, he bent down again, giving her a few more pecks around the corner of her lips.

"You are so beautiful," he said, smiling at her.

Her hands gripped his chain around his neck, pulling him in. "I want you!"

"Let's get cleaned up," Hanjun mumbled into Jade's neck while hugging her from behind.

Jade stood up, and her legs felt like jelly. She managed to walk a few meters before Hanjun picked her up, bridal style. Clinging onto his neck as he opened the bathroom door, he placed her on the black counter.

Turning on the shower, he walked back to her with a smile.

Hanjun placed his hands on her knees, leaning forward and brushing his lips on her neck, which caused her to gasp. Her hands found his hair as he softly kissed her neck and collar bones. A soft groan left his lips while trailing back up to her lips.

"Shower is ready."

He took off his shirt, leading Jade to stare.

"Darling, my eyes are up here."

Blushing, she tried taking off her shirt but failed considering her current state.

"Here, let me help you." Hanjun gently grabbed her shirt, pulling it off her body, his fingers brushing against her body while doing it.

Hanjun was completely undressed and held his hand out. Jade slid herself off the counter, walking to the shower with him. He let her step in and followed her before closing the door.

The water hit her body, and she felt her back relax against Hanjun's torso. His hands caressed her arms and upper back as she leaned on him. His arms wrapped around her, and his chin found her head. Jade put her hands onto his biceps. They stayed in this position letting the water fall on them for a few minutes, enjoying the quiet moment with each other.

Jade woke up feeling all of Hanjun on her backside. Trying to get up, she got grabbed and pulled in a tight grip, forcing her to stay. "Stay," he said, kissing her neck.

She closed her eyes again. "What time is it?" she asked.

"Nine."

"We have to get up, Hanjun," she said, but he kissed her shoulder a few times and then her neck.

"Ten minutes."

"All right, ten minutes," Jade answered, closing her eyes again and moving against him to get comfortable.

"Could someone wake up Jade?" Hanjun asked, while cooking.

"I'll do it," Alex said, giving in to the boys. Alex walked upstairs and knocked two times at Jade's door before he opened it.

"Jade, breakfast in ten. Get ready."

Lifting her head, she focused her eyes to look at Alex.

"Jade?"

"Hm?"

"What a wonderful night, yesterday. Don't you think so?"

113

Jade looked at him, confused, before she got up and dressed herself with one of Hanjun's shirts and black pants. Getting out of the room, she passed Sanghoon.

"Great night, yesterday, huh?" he asked, smiling at her, and Jade got even more confused.

She walked downstairs where all the boys were looking at her and saying loudly, "What a wonderful night, we all had."

And that's when it hits Jade.

She stared at Hanjun with wide eyes, but he was just laughing it off.

He walked over to her and kissed her forehead. "I love that everyone knows you're mine."

"I told you it was a bad idea," she whispered back.

"I have a request," Tai interrupted their whispering.

"Yes?" all of them listened.

"Hanjun and Jade, please, the next time you two fuck, don't do it at this time. There are people who actually want to sleep around this time. Thank you."

"We'll try," Hanjun said, chuckling, pulling Jade in his arms.

Having their weekend off, they decided to go to an amusement park all together. Later, they decided to go to Tai's favorite restaurant for dinner.

"Everyone here?" Joonwoo asked.

Jade can't hold her smile back. Joonwoo is definitely the definition of 'leader' and 'dad'. You can clearly see he knows how to handle kids and, to be honest, the members sometimes act quite like little kids.

Jade wore Hanjun's red hoodie. She styled it like a dress and put shorts under it. With a black jacket, sunglasses, black hat, and a black mask, she looked beautiful and hot at the same time.

The others were dressed all in their own aesthetic, and, if a stranger looks at them, it looks like they're all going to completely different locations.

Jade walked in the middle of the group next to Yoon-Rae when she spotted Hyunwoo and the other bodyguards.

"Guys, this is the last round, all right? We have a reservation we can't miss. Don't forget that," Joonwoo said.

Jade was currently with Yoon-Rae at a candy stall while some of the boys went to their last rollercoaster.

"Mint-Choco?"

"Yes," Jade said, smiling.

"How do you feel after telling them?"

"Actually, very good. It was like something I needed to tell but was too afraid to."

"That's nice."

"And what about you? Are you okay?"

"I'm good, don't worry about me," she said, while taking the ice cream. "Thanks," she said, with a smile to the woman.

"Jade, don't lie to me. You've never teared up since the death of Ae-Cha. You know it is okay to cry. I'm here for you."

"As I said before, I'm good, nothing to worry about." Jade turned coldly around, walking past Yoon-Rae.

"This was such a good dinner," Jade said and stood up.

"Thank you for coming today. I hope we can see you again."

"If we find the time, we would love to come here again," Hanjun added with a smile.

The whole kitchen team was there and bowed at them. "Thanks for coming. We hope you liked it."

"It was wonderful," Alex replied and stood up also. Jade put her cap back on and walked next to Hanjun to their car. Suddenly, they heard camera clicks.

Hanjun reacted instantly, took his jacket off and pulled Jade in it. Right afterward, the bodyguards surrounded them and let them go in their car. "That was close," Hanjun said, while looking at Jade.

"What if they still shot a good picture?"

"I mean everyone knows we are good friends, so it's not the worst thing on Earth."

"But you covered me up so no one would see me, and that is suspicious."

"No, they wouldn't find it suspicious, don't worry."

"Don't worry? Hanjun, I don't—"

"I'll drive," Tai said while closing the door behind him. The boys were divided between the two cars and drove to Jade's house for her upcoming week.

"I'll see you in a week," Hanjun said before he pulled her in for a kiss.

"Yeah, see you then," she said dryly, still upset about earlier.

"Take care."

"I will."

"Are you sure I can't stay overnight?"

"I have to get up very early tomorrow. It is better like this."

"All right," Hanjun sighed. He hugged her tightly before pulling away, smiling.

He pulled her in again and planted a soft kiss on her forehead.

"Hanjun, c'mon!" Si-woo yelled from the car.

"See you in a week. Don't be upset with me then," Hanjun whispered.

She stayed until the car disappeared completely in the dark.

*Hanjun and mysterious girl at a restaurant*
*Jun of B'ONE was seen with a girl. Who is she? Is she his girlfriend?*
*Youngest member of B'ONE was officially seen the first time with his new girlfriend!*
*Has Jun of B'ONE finally found his soulmate?*
*Jun of B'ONE was seen with his new love!*

These were the headlines and hashtags all over social media. Jade had woken up to her phone ringing. **Hanjun <3**
She was currently in a car, next to her is Hyunwoo. He is driving her to a shoot location for her next album.

"Hm?"

"Junghoon and Dowoon will fix this. Don't worry."

"Fix what? What happened?"

"They actually did take pictures yesterday. I'm so sorry."
Jade was silent.
"Darling, please say something."
"Look ..." she took a deep breath. "As you said, our bosses will fix it. Don't worry too much."
"I want to see you."
"You know, I'm out of the city."
"I know. I miss you already."
"I do too. I'll see you in a week, Honey."
"I love you, Darling."
And again, Hanjun hopes to hear the same words coming out of her mouth, but they didn't. She stayed silent as always. He knows he promised Jade he would not push her, but he would give everything to hear those words from her.
"Take care." she replied with instead. Jade hung up and closed her eyes again.
'Why is it so hard to say it? What's wrong with me? Why can't I just say it? It's simple to say these three words in one sentence. He did, too. It's not that hard.'
Jade shook her head to get the bad thoughts out.
Hyunwoo turned his head to her. "Everything all right?"
"Junghoon will fix it."

***

Hanjun pulled her in. One hand behind her back, the other behind her neck. She wraps her arms around his neck. Their lips connect, and they are hypnotized by each other. Once they pulled away, Hanjun put his forehead on hers.
"I've missed you so much.", Hanjun said.
"You taste like peach. Did you change your lip balm?"
"Yeah," Jade said staring in his eyes.
"I like it," he mumbled before he pulled her in for another kiss.
"I got you a present."
"I told you to stop wasting money on me."
"Just come with me," he said, dragging her with him.

# CHAPTER 8

Pulling her to the kitchen, a flower bouquet stood on the counter.
"It was time for some roses, you know."
"I love them."
Turning around, she pulled him in, kissing him as a thank you.
"Get a room. We want to eat later peacefully," Alex said, while cutting the beef for lunch. Jade turned around and said, "Hey" to everyone, before heading to the kitchen to help Alex.
"What happened with the dating rumors?", Tai asked.
"They fixed it, and everything is all right now."
"Please, just—, just be careful. We don't want you guys to get hurt," Joonwoo added before going to his room.

***

"Stop it," Jade mumbled, crawling under the sheets. She shushed Hanjun to his side, rolling over to her side of the bed.
"I've told you many times. I have a limit, and the whole dancing makes my legs shaky. I don't need any more reasons for them not to work. You don't have to make it any harder for me to walk."
Hanjun smirked at her.
"No, stop looking at me like that. That wasn't a compliment at all."
"Well, it sounded like one to me."
Jade stared at him for another few seconds before tossing back over, facing the window and pulling the blanket over her. "Good night, Hanjun."
Jade tried pushing him away, but his grip was too tight for her to open it. She gave up, turned herself to face Hanjun. "What do you want?"
"I want you to let me stay," he sighed.
"Fine, you can stay."
"Thank you, my Love." He kissed her on her cheek, making himself comfortable while putting his head right next to her neck.

"I love you," he mumbled against it. Jade was glad they already turned off the lights because, if not, he would have seen her blushing.

She opened her mouth, trying to say something, "I—" but closed it within a second. Oh c'mon. Just tell him.

"Yes, Love?"

"I'm just tired. That's what I wanted to say."

"Let's sleep," he kissed her softly, trying to hold in his sigh. She doesn't have to hear him wanting to hear the words from her. That's not fair.

*** 

Putting on a flowy blue dress, Jade examined herself in the big mirror. The dress stopped a little higher than her knees, and it was sleeveless. She added some basic white sandals, a white beret, and Hanjun's necklace of his favorite ring with a thin, silver chain through it.

"Coming in," she heard Hyunwoo's voice.

He walked in, and his eyes opened wide.

"Oh my God. I love it. Mum's first impression is important," he said with a grin and a small chuckle. He plopped down on the chair in the dressing room.

"Thank God I've already been there. Now I'm married and never ever have to deal with it again."

"Well, thanks for that," Jade said, while straightening her dress. "How did you even figure it out? We told no one."

"Hanjun blurted it out."

Jade ran her hand through her hair several times.

"Jade, you look cute. Don't stress yourself."

Sighing, she turned to him again.

"You are perfect, Jade. They'll love you."

Heading downstairs, Hanjun sat on the couch and looked up. His eyes widened a bit and a small smile spread across his face. Hanjun was wearing a dark blue suit, with matching dress pants and a white dress shirt under the suit. "Well, it took you long enough. Let's go."

Hyunwoo patted Jade's back, whispering in her ear, "He's totally blown away."

Jade laughed, and he gently pushed her toward him.

"This restaurant is sick. Look at all these things."

They've arrived at Hanjun's mother's restaurant. Hanjun stepped out and opened the door on her side, holding out his hand.

"Wow, such a gentleman."

Jade took his hand as he gave her a smile, closing the door behind her. His other hand found the small of her back, and he led them toward the big door of the restaurant. The restaurant was right next to the sea; it has an amazing view.

The dinner went quickly, and it was time for them to leave. The food was amazing and so was the time they've spent with each other, too.

"Let's go home, Darling."

"You shouldn't drive, Honey. You drank way more than one glass of wine."

"I already called Han-Gyeol, he'll be soon here."

"Hanjun, look good for her. She is the one," his father said, before hugging Jade for the last time.

"Jade, take good care of yourself, and, if anything is bothering you, you'll always be welcomed here."

"Thank you, Mr. Kim."

"It's Seo-Jun for you, my dear." "Thank you, Seo-Jun."

Hanjun hugged Jade from behind and put his chin on her head.

"What if—"

"No one will see us. Let's stay a while like this."

"Everything all right?" she asked.

"Yeah, I'm just happy you like my family."

"Your dad is literally the best and your mother, too."

"I wish I had such a father."

"Now, you've got one."

Jade brushed her fingers on top of his arms, leaning backward into his chest.

What they didn't know is that they were actually seen. Seen by a photographer. The strange man took a lot of pictures before he left quietly. Neither of them heard nor saw him.

# CHAPTER 9

Waking up by wet kisses caused Hanjun to softly moan.
God, how hot is it, to hear a man moan. It's the sexiest thing on
Earth that a man could ever do … Letting her know, she does well.
He turned around, facing Jade with closed eyes. Loving Jade's
touch on him, a smile appeared on his lips. Trying to hold his
moans in, not wanting to sound like a needy dog, he almost failed.
Jade gently stood up and hovers now over him. She sat back
down on his hip, kissing his neck again. His eyes are now open,
full of lust.
Turning her without a problem, he kissed her neck gently before
leaving wet kisses all over it.
Jade arches her back at the kisses, whispering his name.
His lips attached to her lips, leading Jade to open her mouth
completely, giving him access with his tongue. His hands grabbing her waist, pressing her into the bed.
He rested his forehead on hers, rethinking the hot make-out
session. Staring in her lovely eyes caused him to smile.
Gosh, these dimples look so cute, even though his eyes are still
full of lust. Keeping the eye contact, his hand traveled down to
her hips, slightly gripping it.
A gasp left Jade's mouth at the sudden contact. She's already
given up to him. He loves it. He loves the effect he has on her.
Same goes for her. She has such a big effect on him, without
even realizing it much.
Bending down, he started kissing her softly. Leaving some pecks
on her lips, left her desperate for his touch. Starting to deepen the
kisses, leaving wet kisses all over her, she was a moaning mess.
He likes teasing her a lot. The smirk on his face, seeing Jade so
messed up, was irresistible.
He looked so hot teasing her.
Closing her eyes, another moan left her mouth. His grip tightens around her hip, but her hands stopped him—

They trailed up his arms to his shoulders, gripping them hard. Pulling him by them in, she kissed him passionately.

And within a second, she was on top of him. Now, she was the one smirking. Slowly, she started to ride his hips with gentle movements, without a rush. Hanjun gripped onto the bed sheets. He got impatient, wanting her to go faster but she didn't.

Trying to touch her hip and grinding on her, she removed his hands.

"No."

"You touch, I stop."

Pulling him up, she straddled his lap.

"I love you, Jade," he said breathlessly.

Breaking the kiss, Jade hugged him around his neck. Snuggling her head in his neck, a deep chuckle left his mouth. He was drawing different shapes on her back and matched her breathing slowly.

"Thank you," she mumbled.

"For what, Love?" he replied, pitching his voice to hers.

"For not leaving after you found out about my real self," she was close to her tears. Hanjun could feel it and made her look at him.

"Hey, I will never leave you. Don't you dare to think of something like that. I won't. I found my true love, and I'm not leaving her."

"But, but I'm still not fixed."

Tears slowly rolled down her cheek. Hanjun softly kissed them away.

"You don't have to be fixed for being together with me. I love you the way **you are**. Not for anything else. And especially not for your body—

"... although your body is amazing," he added with a smile, giving her a kiss. "I neither love you for your body nor your talent. I love you because of **you**. Do you understand that? You will never get rid of me. You are stuck with me forever."

A smile appeared on her lips, causing her to chuckle. "See? The smile I love the most is back." He kissed her forehead before resting his on hers.

But suddenly, her eyes followed the darkness to the window, staring out of it and slowly her smile faded away.

What is she thinking? Why is she suddenly sad again?

"Everything good?" whispering against her neck, she turned back around.

"Yoon-Rae-"

"I'm worried about him."

"The hate?"

"Hate and Ae-Cha."

"Hanjun, he hasn't been himself anymore since her death. And the hate got more and worse. I'm just worried, he will do ... Do something to himself," she whispered the last part.

"He is stronger than you think, Jade."

Kissing her gently, his hands stayed on her back, drawing heart shapes on it.

"We should sleep," Jade whispered against his lips.

"You're right."

Hanjun laid back down on his back, pulling Jade with him. His hands resting on her lower waist while her head is on his chest, they fell back asleep.

***

Wearing red dungarees with a black shirt in combi and her hair in a bun, added to Jade's cuteness. Hanjun was still asleep in his room.

After she ate her breakfast, she got a text from Yoon-Rae.

*The kids are with Lia. Our fav. Café in thirty?*

*Say no more. <3*

Jade took her keys and drove to the café in Seoul. It was the coffee shop where she got her first Iced Americano. She will never forget that day ever in her life.

The day she met him. Kim Hanjun, the love of her life.

"Boss, I followed her. She's at a café."

"Now she's hugging a man around her age probably, maybe a little older."

"No, it isn't Jun from B'ONE. ... All right, boss. I'll call you when there is any news."

A person completely covered in black clothes stood next to a parking lot in front of the café.

"What would you like, Miss Evans?"

"I'll take my usual, and I have said it several times, just call me Jade," she said, smiling at the waiter.

"Thank you, and you, Mister...?"

"I'm Yoon-Rae, and I'll take an Iced Americano."

Time went by really fast while Yoon-Rae and Jade randomly talked about kids and being a parent. For Jade, kids are a must in her life. She loves kids, and she can't wait to have her own.

"Yes, even with my strict schedule, I would manage it with Hanjun together," she told him.

"Take care, Yoon-Rae," she said, before paying the bill and hugging him tightly.

"I'm always here for you, don't forget that."

"I won't. Take care of yourself," kissing her cheek, he left without another word.

Later that day, Jade went to bed early and couldn't tell Hanjun about it.

The next morning, Jade was walking to the kitchen and recalled their chat yesterday.

Everything happened like Yoon-Rae told her: She won't be awake when he comes home, nor when he goes to work. Yoon-Rae already left, as he told her.

The kids were with Sanghoon and his girlfriend for the weekend as Yoon-Rae told her so.

Jade took a glass and opened the fridge. She walked over to the dinner table where she found a letter with her name on it. Jade recognized the handwriting immediately; it was Yoon-Rae's handwriting. Next to her letter was another letter with B'ONE <3 on it.

\*\*\*

Dear Jade,

Reading this means I have committed suicide.

I'm sorry for putting you in such a situation but I felt unhappy and didn't feel myself getting any better. My reason to live suddenly wasn't alive anymore, and I tried my best, really. I wanted to do it for her, for my kids, for you, but it's so fucking hard.

My days slowly got worse when all I wanted was for them to get better. Everyone always says to wait, and things will get better, but none of them ever seemed to work. You've always been such a good friend to me ... One of my most favorite people in the world. I love you, Jade. But I felt like I was being a burden to you, to my own kids, to my friends. After all, I'm nothing more than a broken mess, screaming to God to finally let me go, to let me meet up with my home, my life, my wife. Why her? Why? I asked him, I asked for forgiveness. What did I do wrong? What did she do wrong to deserve this. But nothing. Not a single answer to it. And after every hate comment I got daily, it feels like my time here is coming to an end.

I have been going to the therapy lessons, and they haven't worked at all. But they have taught me who I truly am.

I'm a person who needs his wife, so it's for the better.

Some people might think, I've had everything I needed, but this isn't true because the thing I need the most was already up here where I am now, finally.

The life I would've lived isn't worth living in ...

... because I'm no one without my wife. I found someone better for our kids than I could have ever been without her, and she knows how much I suffered. Deep inside, I know, she's proud of me.

I could go into detail, explaining why I feel that way, but this note is probably going to be long enough as it is.

To put it simply, I know that I am a person even without my wife but there's a hole in my heart since she left. All the times I looked into my kids' eyes or just at them, they reminded me of her. I never knew there was a word for that feeling, nor was it possible for me to live my life again like I did with her.

I'm not sure what I'm supposed to write in this letter for you because there is so much I could tell you but, in the end, I guess it really doesn't matter.

Do you remember how scared I was of death? Well, now, death doesn't really scare me anymore. I know my kids are safe. My kids will live a wonderful life with you and Hanjun together, I just know it.

I didn't do anything wrong; I believe. I wanted the pain to go away and found a way to be free.

It wasn't my responsibility to go against the world.

It wasn't my path to become world famous.

That's why they say it's hard to go against the world and to become famous.

Why did I even choose this path?

It's quite funny now when I think about it. It's a miracle that I endured through it this whole time.

But I'm sorry I wasn't strong enough to stay and see you and Hanjun get married, have your own kids next to mine, while I would be raising my own kids alone.

I'm sorry for leaving you. I hope in my next life that I don't leave you ever again, and trust me, it was hard, hard to decide but still, not hard at all. The desire of seeing my love again was stronger, the hate of the people was stronger, the voices in my head were stronger.

I'm really glad I had you in my life, despite it ending so quickly. But I feel like my happiness ended with Ae-Cha's death, and only pain lied ahead of me. I tried to think positive, to believe I can raise my kids on my own, but everything reminded me of her. I can barely look into the eyes of my kids and not see her.

I don't want to hurt you, or anybody, so please forget about me. Just try. Find yourself a better friend. Everyone moves on after death, and, after they're done grieving, I'm sure things will turn out fine, unlike with me. I just couldn't endure the pain, the grieving after her. There was no way I could have survived this without her. I'm just not capable enough to go on further without her, and all the rejection, the hate, the failure in my life has shown me that it is the truth.

You ought to know that you were my best friend. I know we had a rough start but actually, I love you, Jade. You were my best friend. You really were. I know you loved me, and I loved you.

No one should have gone through what you went through, but you did. And it kills me to think of it.

But I didn't love you the way you loved me. I don't hate you for that. It just makes me sorry that I'm not your second Hanjun. The person who loves you the way you should be loved.

I know when you think about how I went, you'll get it.

Since she left, it was always uneasy to be alive. The idea of being dead makes me feel clear, the idea of being together with her. When I thought of it, it made me think of peace, peace, and peace. It made me happy. Happy to be with her again. And happy to see my kids grow up with the love they need. I could never give them the love they need because there would always be a piece missing, my piece.

I'm looking forward to it, seeing her, the love of my life, again. I want you to be happy for me, that this is better for me. That I found what I needed. I know you won't be but please try. Because it's the last thing I wish before I'll leave. You happy.

Now, that I'm gone, you don't have to worry anymore about me. Just know, that I'm happy with her.

The daily Blue and Grey, it was just not for me. I wanted to get out of it. To leave this color palette but as much as I tried, nothing helped. I tried, I tried so hard. Trying to ignore the voices, the desire, thinking it was just a way out of all but at the end of the day, where was my angel? Where is my angel now? Someone should come and save me please. And when I thought about my angel, I knew exactly where it was. Up here, here where I am now. But your angel isn't up here. Trust me. Your angel is right next to you carrying the name Kim Hanjun. He is your Angel, and she is mine.

I know everyone is happy. I tried to be happy for you, for them. Can you even look at me? How broken I am? I'm literally drowned in Blue and Grey. I hid all things behind it. My laughter, the meaning of my tears, all behind the colors blue and grey. I didn't see any other color in my world. It's just Blue and Grey, and I'm sick of it. My world became blue and grey, the moment she left.

Maybe that's why I've been living so hard. But standing here, in the middle of the hate, looking back when I was the happiest person ever, it didn't match. She wasn't there. Whether it was anxiety or depression, it's me who's lonely. I just wanna be happier, I want you to be happier, I want them to be happier.

There used to be days when I thought I was doing okay, or at least that I was going to be. We'd be hanging out somewhere, and everything would just fit right, and I would think, 'It will be okay if it can just stay like this forever,' but, of course, nothing can ever stay just how it is forever. What more can I say? Just tell me 'Good Job'. 'You did great'. Tell me, I suffered enough. Even though you can't laugh right now, just don't send me off blaming me or you.

Please, don't mourn long for me. Live your life further. Live it with all my pride. I don't want you to mourn long, for real. Less than a week is okay, afterward no. Just no. I know, you can live a life without me. Think about the time, you didn't know me. You lived, right? Live like that again. As soon as you accept my death, the better it is for you. Don't blame yourself for this or the others. It was my decision, and I did it because I knew my kids will have a great family. And after all that will happen, your Spring Day will come back to you, no matter what. Trust me.

Goodbye,
Your Seo Yoon-Rae

Jade burst into tears out loud. Trying to reach the counter with her hand, she failed and fell.

She didn't bother standing up. She just sat there. But her crying increased massively. It got worse and worse. Jade was crying so bad, she could barely breathe, and, with her sight blurred, she tried to take the smaller letter out of the envelope. Failing, she cried even harder. Feeling the tears streaming down her face to her shoulders and hitting her clothes, she couldn't believe it. He is dead. It's not possible.

How can he just leave her alone? Alone in this world. She can't make it without him. He was there for her.

She isn't ready to be a mother yet. She can't take care of two kids.

Hearing the sound of her, his loved one, crying, he ran downstairs. Hanjun was wearing his black jogger pants without a top and his hair were messy.

Stopping at the bottom of the stairs, trying to figure out where she is, he could hear her clearly.

Kneeling on the dining room floor, crying, she looked awful. A crying mess, not letting herself catch her own breath. Seeing her there broke his heart. She hasn't cried like this in a while. No, actually, Hanjun has never seen her cry like this.

The last time was back in England, the day her father tried to rape her. Hyunwoo saw it. No one else. He was the only one and now? Hanjun was the second one. Seeing her at the worst she's ever been.

"Love, what's wrong?"

He ran toward her when he saw the letter with B'ONE on the table.

Same as Jade, he knew exactly from who it was. But right now, he didn't care.

He only cares about Jade right now.

She put her hand over her mouth to stop her loud crying but after a few seconds, she removed it and fell into Hanjun's arms. Still, he didn't know what was going on. His hand was rubbing soothingly up and down Jade's back as he pressed her against his chest. Hanjun closed his eyes for a second and hugged her closely, while he took the letter from her. Jade didn't do anything and let him do it.

She twisted her legs around his hips and buried her head in his neck while Hanjun started reading the letter.

Hanjun slowly dropped the letter and hugged her tightly. Jade moved her hands to his neck and pulled him closer. However, he managed to stand up with her. They are still hugging each other with a warm embrace. No one let go. They stayed like this very long, before Hanjun softly pulled away. He bent down and picked up the letter with the envelope and looked inside.

Jade stood there, staring into space.

Unfolding the small paper, he held his breath.

***

You'll be the perfect family!

I've never doubted Hanjun's skills as the godfather of Dae-Jung, and I've also never doubted your skills as the godmother of Jin-Ae. Please let them have a mother and a father.

Don't let them forget us. <3

***

Hanjun held his tears, turning around but Jade wasn't there anymore—

In the same moment, he heard a door shutting. Jade must've gone upstairs while he was reading. He ran upstairs and stopped in front of Jade's room.

Jade was sitting behind the locked bedroom on her bed. Covering herself under her blanket, she didn't want to see anyone.

"Darling, come out, please. I'm here for you," Hanjun sighed and leaned his forehead against the door. He slowly fell to the floor on the other side of the room.

"Please, Please, just don't hurt yourself," his voice broke. He couldn't hold the tears anymore and broke down. As his crying stopped for a few seconds, he messaged the boys.

*Please, come to Jade's house. It's about Yoon-Rae. Now! It is very important.*

The boys arrived all together and saw the door open. They started to run faster and finally reached the table with the letter on it. Kai opened their letter slowly.

"What happened?" Joonwoo asked, who was standing right in front of him.

"Yoon-Rae, he's-, he's-. He... is...dead," Kai whispered quietly falling to his knees. The boys stared at him in disbelief.

Joonwoo stood up after a few hours. Hanjun wasn't there and so wasn't Jade. He walked around and then upstairs to find Hanjun sitting in front of Jade's room.

His jogger pants, completely wet of his crying and his upper naked body was shining due to it.

His hair was still messy and his eyes red and puffy. Hanjun instantly wiped his tears away, trying not to show that he is hurt. Joonwoo hugged him tightly and long. "It is okay to be hurt, Hanjun. That's okay."

"Where is Jade?" he whispered. "She locked herself in her room." "The boys are all downstairs, waiting. You guys ready?"

"Give me a minute with her alone. We will go down afterward," Joonwoo nodded and walked downstairs.

"Jade?" Hanjun asked in front of the door. "He did a good job. Yoon-Rae did great, and he suffered enough."

There was nothing but silence for a couple of minutes before the door opened gently. Jade's eyes were all red, puffy, and full of tears. Hanjun pulled Jade to him. "He suffered enough, and he did amazing," he whispered again in her ears. Jade tried to convince herself that he is actually dead but still, she can't accept it.

'He left her. Left her alone in this world. She needs him. She can't live without him. Why did he leave? Why? Just why? It's not fair.' Hanjun wanted to pull away, but her grip got tighter. "I'm here. It's okay."

Her crying started to get worse again, and she began to feel dizzy.

The grip around Hanjun got looser until her hands suddenly dropped down. Hanjun got scared and broke their hug.

Jade's eyes were closed, and she didn't move. He lifted her up and immediately called the boys from downstairs. They rushed upstairs and saw Jade lying in Hanjun's arms.

"What happened?"

"Call an ambulance. She fainted."

Jade woke up in the hospital. She stared at the ceiling when her head started to hurt again. She heard the boys next to her talking indistinctly. Hanjun glanced over and saw her awake.

"Jade, you're awake." He immediately rushed to her, holding her hand tightly.

The door opened, and Sanghoon was there. He stood there confused; next to him were Yoon-Rae's kids. Dae-Jung knew immediately something was wrong.

"Where is daddy?" he asked, worried.

"Where is daddy?" he repeated the same question again. Picking him up to her bed, Jade brushed the hair out of his face. "Your daddy is now with your mummy up there," she whispered quietly.

"He left?" Dae-Jung mumbled.

Nodding her head, she saw Sanghoon walking next to Eric with red eyes. Hanjun took Jin-Ae and let Sanghoon fall into the arms of Joonwoo.

Sanghoon read the whole letter and glared into space. Tai noticed it and stood up, walked over to him, and hugged him tightly. No one spoke a word.

Junghoon closed the door behind him, walking with his head down toward them. Putting a hand on Jade's shoulder, he looked up. "Yoon-Rae was found in his house. He took an overdose," he said quietly.

"C-can I see him?" Sanghoon mumbled. Junghoon nodded and Sanghoon followed him. He was the only one who wanted to see him at the moment, and that's okay. Everyone deals with the death of a loved person differently.

\*\*\*

Jae's wife stood up to bring everyone a glass of water when she heard the doorbell ring.

"I'll go," Tai mumbled.

His wife touched his shoulder to urge him not to go. Kissing her forehead, he stood up slowly. His feet carried him to the door. Sanghoon was back with Junghoon and Dowoon. They all got in and walked next to Tai into the living room. The boys were all sitting on the big couch in Jade's house. Each of them with their loved person. All except Eric, his wife was still abroad, but she'll take the next possible flight to come home. She canceled her whole schedule and dropped everything to get to Eric as soon as possible. Their children were playing in another room, not exactly knowing what happened.

It was already late, and the message got spread to a few artists who were close with Yoon-Rae and to all the idols who worked in the same company. All of them canceled their schedule due this terrifying news and the closest one even visited B'ONE and Jade. Now, all of them were on their way back home.

"I'll go get the kids," said Sanghee, Joonwoo's wife.

"Me too, they have to go to bed," Yu Yan, Tai's wife, agreed and also stood up.

They both wanted to walk to the other room when Junghoon stopped them.

He looked back to the boys and Jade who just sat there in their own thoughts on the couch, "I think you all should sleep here, there are enough rooms for all of you."

Sanghee looked back to Joonwoo, who started to cry again. Walking back to him, she hugged him tightly. "That would be good, I think."

"Papa, Daddy, all good?" Jintara asked Malee. "We have to take good care of him, all right?"

Jintara nodded and took Malee's hand in hers.

"Will we sleep here?"

Malee nodded and walked with Arak in his other hand behind Junghoon, who showed them their room.

"I thought we could all write something to Yoon-Rae, walk to the fireplace in the forest next to the neighborhood and let him go—" Alex said quietly. "You know what, never mi—"

"No, I would love to do it," Jade replied with a whisper. Alex looked at her with red eyes and a soft smile.

Putting on their jackets, Jade was the last one who got outside and closed the door behind her.

She looked up and saw Hanjun. He waited for her at the door while the others waited at the gate. A small smile appeared on his lips, not reaching his eyes though. They were red and puffy. He stretched his hand out, and Jade took it hesitantly.

"Let's go. He is waiting," he whispered.

After walking for almost an hour, they reached the forest and the fireplace. They waited a few minutes to let the fire grow before all of them put their letters into the big fire. The boys and Jade surrounded the fire and stared into the flames.

"We will miss you," Hanjun said quietly.

Jade joined. "You suffered enough."

"You did a good job."

"We are proud of you."

Everyone said one thing before they stared back into the flames. Eric's wife wasn't here yet, but she was on her flight, finally. She will be here in about three hours. Hannah is also on her way home to stay back in Korea. She was done with her job in L.A. and decided to come back, although she hadn't planned to be back this soon.

After a few hours, they still stood outside around the fire, but it got much colder outside.

"Let's go back," Kai said and looked into the fire pit. All agreed and extinguished the fire. Without talking, they walked back.

Malee was lying on the bed facing the window when Si-woo got in. Si-woo didn't change his clothes and went straight to bed. Malee felt the bed dips beside him, but he wasn't pulled into Si-woo's chest like usual.

Si-woo laid in bed without even touching him a bit. Malee turned slowly around and pulled Si-woo to his chest, patting his head gently.

Si-woo buried his face in Malee's neck while hugging him tighter. "It's okay, Darling. I'm here," Malee whispered and kissed his forehead. Si-woo cried out loud while grabbing Malee's white shirt.

Mei Zhen sat on the bed scrolling through her phone. She was already in her seventh month. Only two months are left before the birth of her twins. As soon as she heard Alex come in, she dropped her phone and sat up. Alex's eyes were red and puffy. His whole body was like numb, and he didn't bother to look up. Alex walked over to the bed, sitting down. Mei Zhen crawled to him, hugging him tightly for a long time.

Jae opened the door and was hugged tightly by Jihoo, "It's okay. I'm here for you."
Jae closed his eyes and cried on Jihoo's shoulder. She slowly walked to the bed and lay down on it. Jihoo kept stroking his hair as he laid on her chest.
"Try to sleep for a few hours, all right?" she whispered. "I'll watch over you."

Closing the door quietly, Hannah walked in.
Sophie was already with Eric in their room, probably helping him sleep.
All the members were upstairs in their own rooms, except Jade.
Jade sat on the floor, with her phone next to her as she stared at the wall.
"Hey," Hannah whispered.
Jade's head didn't turn. She didn't even bother to move.
Hannah put her things down and walked around the couch to stand in front of her. Glaring at her, Jade looked into her eyes. Hannah's heart stopped for a moment. Instantly, she kneeled down to Jade, hugging her tightly.
Jade didn't move.
She didn't hug back.
She didn't say anything.
She didn't do anything.

Something was odd. It was strange. Jade was strange. She lost someone she loved but earlier she was quite touchy with Hanjun. Why not now? Why not with her best friend?

Hannah pulled away and dragged Jade behind her upstairs. Without fighting back, Jade followed Hannah.

Knocking slightly at the door of Jade's bedroom, Hannah opened it. Hanjun laid in bed, his eyes were open, staring at the mirror. His head lifted up a bit when he heard them. Hannah dragged Jade to Hanjun before she whispered goodbye and went to her room.

Hanjun pulled Jade in for a hug and, again, Jade didn't hug him back. Her body felt numb.

Waking up, she was still in his arms. Jade gently removed his hands and let the darkness surround her. She shrugged over to the edge of the bed and, after a long time, she fell asleep again.

Hanjun's eye opened one by one due to the bright sunlight. Jade was on the edge of the bed, between them a huge space. He stretched his arm out and touched her waist softly.

She flinched a bit, even though she was still asleep, and it made him worried.

Immediately, he sat up and moved closer. Seeing her face, dry tears were on her cheeks. She cried herself into sleep, Hanjun guessed.

Hanjun tucked a hair behind her ear when her eyes opened. She moved away from him as if she was scared by him.

"I'm sorry, I didn't want to scare you, Darling," he whispered.

"I'll let you sleep," Hanjun stood up and closed the door behind himself, letting her be alone.

# CHAPTER 10

Jade stayed in her bed for nine days after his death.

While the members **accepted** his death, like Yoon-Rae told them to do. She couldn't accept his death. Jade couldn't accept the fact that he's not here anymore. Not in the room next to hers, not in his house, not in the dorm. He's not here anymore. He is now up there. And as much as she wishes him to be happy, she still feels betrayed. He left without a word. He didn't talk to her about all the pain he felt.

Every day, she talks with him. Asking him why, why her. She felt better talking with him than with the members or Hanjun. They're just gonna try to tell her it wasn't her fault.

But Yoon-Rae, he just listens like always. It was one of the things he was really good at. Just being there and listening to all her struggles. Sometimes, people need a good listener rather than someone who gives advises.

The awards show, which was planned for September third wasn't held. No one was ready to perform two days after such a painful loss of a loved one, a member, a friend or just someone who everyone knew. Instead, they decided to do the awards show at the end of September with both B'ONE and Jade taking part in it.

Every morning, Hanjun opens the door to see how she's doing but all he sees is her puffy eyes staring at the floor. She neither looks at him nor through the window, even though it's her comfort zone; she would always look out the window to help comfort herself. She loves to look through windows. Hanjun could hear her some days talking to him. It made him feel a bit less worried. At least she's talking with someone, even if this someone isn't himself.

Jade was barely sleeping and, if Hanjun didn't force her, she wouldn't eat at all.

During the nine days, she barely spoke to Hanjun, even though he tried again and again to talk to her, to understand her pain, to help her, to listen to what she's saying, to be there for her.

"Jade, Love, you need to get up and take a shower."
She hadn't showered in days, and the room already started to smell bad.
"No," she answered without even looking at Hanjun.
"Love, c'mon. It's not healthy."
"Stop caring about me. I don't need you."
"I don't wanna argue with you. You're not in a good condition and neither am I. Please, get up and take a shower or else, I'm gonna drag you myself."
"You wouldn't."
It was the first time she looked at him in days.
"Oh yes, I will. Believe me."
Jade stared hesitantly before she finally got up, walking with quick steps to the bathroom. She closed the door right behind her, leaving him in the room. He took the opportunity to open the windows, change the sheets, and get her clothes ready for the day.
Sitting on the bed, Hanjun thought about what he could do to get her back. To find his love, his Jade, the woman who opened up to him and talked about every mistreatment she went through, trusted him, and isn't afraid to answer him. It hurts Hanjun to see her shutting down on him.
After a few minutes, she came back into the room with a towel around her body and wet hair. Jade walked quickly to get her clothes and went back into the bathroom, but she went so fast, that she forgot her bra.
Heading to the bathroom with it, he opened the door—
Jade sat on the floor, a little blade was in her hand — probably one from his razor — and a few cuts covered her wrist.
As soon as she heard him, she dropped the blade, stood up and walked away from Hanjun as if she was afraid of him. Hanjun immediately followed her.

Jade stopped at the window, sitting on the couch, staring through the window. Her hands were in front of her body, not showing the cuts.

Hanjun just stood there, letting her know he was there. Not touching her, not speaking to her. His breath was calm, but he was scared. Scared of losing her.

"You've been through a lot. No wonder you're hurt."

"I'm still here and want to help you find a way to cope which won't hurt you anymore, my Love," Hanjun whispered gently, but stayed still, without touching her.

"I'm sorry," she mumbled without looking at him.

"Hey, look at me," Hanjun said while kneeling down in front of her, still not touching her. He noticed a tear had fallen on her cheek as she stared at him in shock.

"I'm sorry. I didn't mean to cry," her voice was a whisper, and she bit her lip wiping her cheek. He furrowed his eyebrows at her.

"Jade, it's okay to be vulnerable with me. I'm never gonna judge you," he softened his expressions and reached for her hand, but took it back, glancing at her. She slightly nodded her head, and he placed his hand on top of hers. Her teary eyes stared at him.

She's quiet, just staring at him chewing on her bottom lip.

"I knew he would do it. It's all my fault." She removed her hand from under his and used it to conceal the sobs escaping her mouth. She turned her head away from him so he didn't see her face.

Hanjun has never been the best at comforting with words, but he always found a way with Jade. He gentled grabbed her wrist and led her to turn toward him. Jade's face was filled with sadness, and it broke him.

"Come here," his hand gestured for her to come to him. Hanjun sat on the couch as she moved over and wrapped her legs around his torso while nuzzling her head into his neck, letting her arms fall over his shoulders before she started crying again.

This time, it was filled with more sadness than before, more emotions. Hanjun stroked her hair and wrapped his hands around her waist.

"He gave me hints, but I was just too dumb to see them," her voice broke into sobs once again. Hanjun didn't tell her to calm down or anything because she needed to get this all out before she might do the same to herself.

"What if I can't be a mother? What if I'm not ready? What if I disappoint him?" her crying continued and, with each sob, he held her tighter, making sure she felt safe. Jade gripped onto him tighter, and her words broke Hanjun.

He knew exactly how much Jade overthinks, about her crying once he 'falls' asleep and her nightmares. But on top of all of that, he knew exactly how it felt, because Yoon-Rae talked to him, too. He gave him so many hints but, same as Jade, he didn't get them.

After she cried for a while, no other words were said. She gripped his shirt when the pain got worse, and her sobs were loud but muffled because of his clothed shoulder.

Drawing tiny hearts on the bottom of her back seemed to calm her down, like always. These tiny hearts are something Hanjun automatically does if she needs comfort.

She rested her head on Hanjun's shoulder when a quiet sob left Hanjun's mouth. Jade's head lifted immediately. Looking into his eyes, shock was placed on her face. Staring back without a word, he looked so broken.

"I'm a good listener, you know ..." she whispered in his ears.

"Y-Yoon-Rae talked with me, too, Jade," his voice also broke down into a sob. "He gave me so many hints, but I was just too stupid to not get them," his crying got harder, and his grip around Jade got tighter. "I could have stopped him. He's dead because I was—"

"He's now reunited with Ae-Cha," she whispered, softly, stroking his hair like he did to her a few minutes ago.

"I just think, I could have changed it."

"No one could have done that. It was his decision to do it, only to be with Ae-Cha."

"But I need him."

"He's suffered enough. Let him go," she muttered, also crying. "Let him go," she repeated herself a few times.

141

She was right. He needs to let him go. But she needs to do it, too. It's time to live the life Yoon-Rae wants for them; he specifically asked them to live. But can she actually live with the fact that he isn't here anymore?

Some might think that two weeks are not enough to mourn and accept the death of a person, but well, they didn't know Yoon-Rae. Yoon-Rae doesn't like to mourn and, especially after the death of Ae-Cha, he started to hate it. It only breaks people, in his opinion. He doesn't want that to happen with the boys and Jade. He wants them to live a good life with all of his pride, accepting what happened. It's easier to live the life he tells you to rather than living it without him telling you.

***

Rubbing his eyes, he looked around. Jade wasn't lying next to him. Hanjun got up, stretching himself and yawned for a few times before he opened the door. Walking downstairs, he heard someone talking.

"Jade, there are photos of you everywhere on the internet!" the voice yelled. Jade didn't answer.

"How the fuck did this happen?!"

"Jade, I'm talking to you. Answer me, God damn it!"

"I don't know," Jade whispered. Hanjun could hear that she was scared.

"How could this happen? I thought I was clear when I told you it was okay."

"I'm... I'm sorry."

"Shut up, that won't help!" the voice got even louder, and Jade flinched at the loud voice.

Hanjun rushed around the corner, touching her arm gently. Jade turned around with another flinch. Her face instantly relaxed as she saw Hanjun. He pulled her in and faced him.

"How dare you? How dare you to talk like this to her. Don't you know what happened?! Screaming at her won't help."

"It's all her fault. If she wasn't with you, there would be no such big mistake."

"Say that again. I dare you! If she wasn't with me, I wouldn't even be here anymore. So **shut the fuck up**!"

Dowoon flinched at Hanjun's voice. "I'm sorry, Hanjun. It's just, there is so much to do right now with the death of Yoon-Rae—"

"Don't talk about his death."

"I'm sorry. There are just too many things going on, and I over-reacted and didn't know what to do and then there is the awards show we still need to attend. It's a bit hard for everyone."

"Better for you," Hanjun stroked Jade's back while talking to Dowoon.

The newest pictures showed Jade and Hanjun at the day of Yoon-Rae's funeral. The pictures were taken in front of Jade's mansion. But there were lots more pictures not on the same day. It showed Jade and Hanjun when they were out, sometimes the boys were with them, sometimes not.

"Jade, Darling. Why don't you go upstairs, to sleep a bit longer, huh?"

"Hm," Jade whispered, not looking into his eyes. He kissed her forehead before he let her go upstairs.

Hanjun faced Dowoon again when he heard quiet sobs. Recognizing it, he immediately turned around. "Let's discuss this later."

Dowoon wanted to reply, but Hanjun was already upstairs without waiting for an answer. Dowoon felt it, too. He has never talked in this tone with Dowoon but since his death ... everything changed. He shut down any emotions he has, except for Jade.

***

Hanjun got out of the company very late. It was already past midnight, around 2 a.m.

About three weeks ago, the first photos of Jade and Hanjun got leaked but it didn't stop. Every day, there were new pictures of them.

The company still tries to shut down everything, but there is this one specific photographer who takes all these pictures. They've even integrated the police because this was much more than just stalking. Although the company found a perpetrator, they aren't sure yet. They have to wait until he posts something again.

Hanjun walked down the street when a car followed him slowly... Since these pictures were leaked, Hanjun gets much hate from Jade's admirers.

Most of them were male but still, there were also a few female 'fans', and while he got hate from them, Jade got the hate from *his* admirers.

The difference was clearly seen; mostly female go after her but still a few males also.

Both of them got and still get lots of death threats and lots of bad comments on photos of them. It's miserable.

Yoon-Rae's funeral was several weeks ago, and, of course, there were still pictures everywhere on the internet of Jade and Hanjun. And since the funeral, it got worse day by day.

Hanjun started to get concerned and looked around him to see if there was anyone there. There wasn't; he was alone.

The car still followed him when Hanjun turned left to a public place, but, unfortunately, there was no one at the place, so he was still alone.

Hearing the car door shut, he started to walk faster. But, after a few seconds, he was surrounded by a few men.

"Hello, Hanjun," one of them said.

"Finally, we see each other face to face."

"Who are you?"

"Don't you remember us?"

"What do you want?"

"Nothing but you," one of them spoke up. Hanjun didn't answer. A man walked up to him and touched his arm. He pulled it away harshly.

"Chill, we only want to play a bit with you."

Hanjun could smell the alcohol on their breath.

Another man suddenly picked up a thick branch that laid on the street next to a tree. Fortunately, Hanjun had quick reflexes and could catch the first few hits of it, but he got weaker with every hit.

The other men picked also branches up and began to hit him.

"That's for touching the love of my life," one said, while hitting him on the back.

"That's for even looking at her."

"How dare you! She belongs to me!"

Hanjun could barely breathe while trying to hold himself up. A man kicked him in his stomach. Another punched him in his face.

"When we are done, you won't be as handsome as you were," they said, laughing.

Hanjun's nose was bleeding, his temple had several cuts from the branches, his lips were full of blood, and he wasn't sure if it came from his lips or out of his mouth. His clothes had slight cuts in them and were drenched with a few drips of his own blood while his body was marked with bruises.

Hanjun opened the door quietly, putting on the hoodie, which laid next to the shoes.

Fortunately, only Eric was downstairs watching TV.

"You're back. Ready to watch our movie?"

"Hm," he just replied and sat next to Eric, not looking at him. After a while Hanjun turned slowly to Eric. "I'm going to bed," Hanjun said in a weak tone.

"Already? I thought we would watch this movie to end." "I'm really tired, Eric. Sorry."

Hanjun almost fell down while he stood up from the couch. When he started to walk, he felt dizzier and lost his balance again. Eric immediately stood up and caught him before he fell to the floor. Eric said something, but Hanjun couldn't hear him — everything went black.

***

Hanjun woke up on his bed, under the blanket.

Hearing the boys talking outside his room, he searched for the one voice. Isn't she there? Where is she?

He tried to sit up, but it was still hurting. That's when a knock was on his door.

After a quiet, "yes," the door opened, and Jade was there. She came in and closed the door behind her.

"Who did this?" she asked, concerned and walked over to him. She sat on the edge of the bed on his side.

"It's nothing. Don't worry."

She asked again, "Who did this?"

"It's not that bad," Hanjun sat up and faced her. Everything hurt, but he tried not to show it. Jade asked a few times again, but there was always the same answer.

"Why do you always do this, Hanjun?"

Hanjun was now standing in front of her. Jade shoved him back by his chest. His face twitched due to the pain. Jade tried to ignore it but failed a bit with her concerned sight at him.

"Why do you always have to run away from your problems when you have people who can help you?"

"**Who**?!"

Jade flinched at his tone, taking one step back when he moved one step forward.

"Who do I have, huh?"

"**Me**!" Jade matched his tone, silencing the rest of what he was saying. "You've always had me," she then whispered, looking down at the floor.

"You're the one who pushes me away when I try to help you. You do this with everyone," she folded her arms, hugging herself. "I always tried to help, but since the photos—"

"Jade—"

"I am your girlfriend, Hanjun. I am your best friend, Hanjun," she cut him off, tears lined her eyes, but she forced them away because she wasn't about to cry in front of him. Not today, she won't cry today just because she feels guilty about what happened.

"I let you into my life. Let you see what broke me. I was always there to take care of you. I just wish you would realize that," Jade sighed, turning around and walking back to the seat on the desk in his room, where she rubbed her eyes. Her nose stung as tears threatened to escape.

And not a single word escaped him. She furiously rubbed her nose with the back of her hands to try and avoid crying.

"Jade."

She didn't answer.

"Jade," he sighed, "Come here."

"No."

"Jade, come here, please," his tone ... desperate.

"No," she replied again.

She heard him exhale loudly, his footsteps growing louder when she felt his presence right behind her.

"What do you want from me, Jade?"

She sighed, exhausted from this conversation, "I want to help you. I want to help you like you help me."

Jade slightly looked over her shoulder, seeing his broad body standing there. "But you never let me."

There was silence. It was until she felt his fingertips under her chin turning her head to the side to face his slightly. The sudden touch made her heartbeat faster.

"Why do you want to help me so badly?" his voice tiredly rasped out. "What do you see in me that's worth saving, Jade?"

"Everything about you is worth saving, Hanjun."

When Jade said that, his entire world stopped. It's like he has been craving to hear those words all his life but never knew how much he needed them until today, especially from her.

"You just don't realize it yet," she whispered sadly, a small smile that didn't quite reach her eyes as her eyes twinkled at him. She turned around fully.

"Why do you think I can't handle it alone?"

Jade stared into his eyes, "I don't think you can't handle it alone. I just don't want you to handle it alone. I don't wanna let you feel the way I felt. I want you to have a person who you can trust and who's there for you. I want to be the person who lets you feel okay about not being okay."

Hanjun didn't say anything. Slowly his hand wrapped around her body, hugging her tightly. His grip got tighter as soon as he started to cry.

Jade stood there, hugging him, and rubbing her hands soothingly up and down his back.

"Did it happen on the street?"

"Yeah."

"When?"

"When I left the company, they followed me, and then they did it."

"Why didn't you tell the—"

"I'm not really okay to be not okay around them right now."

'The death changed him, too. He turned colder to anyone except her,' Jade could feel it.

"And around me?" she asked.

"Since I've met you, you were always the person who let me feel it."

"But why didn't you tell me strai—"

"I didn't want you to worry about it."

"Hanjun, you fainted and lost blood."

"About that, I am starting to feel dizzy again."

"C'mon, let's get you to the bed." Jade took his hand softly and walked with him over to the bed. "You need to rest."

"Jade?"

"Hm?"

"Are you okay?"

"Why?"

"I, I saw the comments," he sighed. That's when a tear left Jade's eye. Hanjun pulled her toward him, letting her cry as much as she needed. She grabbed his shirt tightly, crying into his chest. He didn't let go, still patting her head softly.

"Did you talk to Yoon-Rae?"

Nodding her head, he kissed it. "That's good, Jade."

"Talk to him, he will listen."

"Hanjun?"

"Yes, Love?"

Taking a deep breath, she looked up and boldly said, "I love you."

She did it. She finally said it.

Kissing her gently, pulling her against his chest, he smiled in between each.

"Can you say it again?"

"I love you, Kim Hanjun."

Snuggling his head in her neck, he left several kisses.

"I love you, Jade."

QY Entertainment did its job right. Two articles, about the rumors of Jade's and Hanjun's relationships and the current state of Hanjun were posted by the end of the week.

Hanjun's current state was bad; with his injuries, he will not be able to perform at the upcoming awards ceremony. The offenders were already found by the Label and the police.

Getting punished for what they did, a lot of the fans were glad they were found. And the man who uploaded the pictures has also been caught and now has a big problem.

***

"Papa, Daddy is crying again," Jintara said, dragging Malee to their room.

The members and Jade decided to stay in their mansion with their families, to be with each other since the death of Yoon-Rae.

Kneeling down, Malee ran his hands through Jintara's hair, "Could you stay with Jade for a while?"

"Why is Daddy crying?"

"You know, he lost someone who's very important to him. Let us be alone for a while, okay?"

Jintara nodded slightly and ran downstairs to find Jade in the kitchen.

***

The day of the awards show is here. Sadly, Jade and Hanjun couldn't perform their choreography together due to Hanjun's injuries, but Jade's performance with the boys was amazing.

The show came to an end, and B'ONE got the last big award of the show. They won it with the song that Yoon-Rae produced and wrote for them about their friendship; it brought memories back for them all.

Everyone had tears in their eyes as they walked up to the stage, taking the award.

"This one is for you, Yoon-Rae!" Eric yelled into the mic. Holding the trophy up in the air, he gave it a kiss. Like every time, each of the boys gave a short speech.

They talked mostly about Yoon-Rae, about the good moments with him, the memories and the years they had with each other. Jade stood the whole time, clapping after every speech, her eyes full of tears, but she looked beautiful.

Sanghoon was the last one. Sanghoon was Yoon-Rae's best friend and neighbor in Thailand and when Yoon-Rae's family wasn't there, he became a part of Sanghoon's family.

Holding the award tightly around his fingers, he started speaking into the mic. "Wow, I've worried so much before coming on this stage again tonight. Standing on stage for this last award, we all know what it's about, and I was honestly really scared."

He took a deep breath. "Before I start, I would like to bring someone onto the stage. Some people might not believe it, but this person suffered as much as we did." He pointed at his members behind him. "She was close with him, although they had a rough start. But since then, everything changed for them. They started to produce things together, spending more time with each other, and caring about each other. I think, she deserves as much as we did to come up to this stage again."

He stepped away from the mic, gave Si-woo the award and ran off the stage. The camera followed him, showing every move on the big screen. He walked up to Jade, smiling at her. Sanghoon hugged her tightly before pulling her up the stage.

Making room for Jade, Jade stood between Jae and Tai. Not wanting to confirm any of the rumors with Hanjun.

"On May 7, 2009, through our company, I was able to meet one of the most caring people in the world, named Seo Yoon-Rae. It wasn't hard to like him. He was the sweetest guy I've ever met. We made a promise that day. To make sure that both of us will debut. To debut together, in the same company and in the same group."

"In our early trainee days, we found out that we were neighbors back in Thailand, and we got even closer. Yoon-Rae didn't have his family back then in South Korea, and he lived with me. Together, we made it to the group B'ONE, and we promised each other to not let go. To stay together until the rest of our days. We wanted to visit the world, together as best friends and as a family but—" his voice broke. "But, unfortunately, he left us a few weeks ago. The pain is still here, and I don't think I will ever recover from this, but I let him go. It's the thing Yoon-Rae told us to do. To live a life with his full pride."

He said, "Yoon-Rae told me, I cannot blame myself for it, but sometimes I feel like as if it's my fault for not seeing it. Not seeing the signs he gave out. I know he will find his peace, and I know he will always watch us from up there." Tears streamed down his face, blurring his view.

The audience had tears in their eyes, clapping for him. He took a step forward again, pulling the mic to him. "Yoon-Rae, I'll make sure you'll always be remembered by everyone. I won't forget you, my friend."

The camera showed each member crying for their loss. It hits even harder seeing Jade crying the most. Her eyes were already red and puffy again, tears streaming her face down. She tried wiping them away, but her hands were shaking, and honestly, it wasn't fair of the camera men to show them on the big screen, crying for their loss.

Jade's tiny hand tried again to wipe her tears away, but Hanjun was faster. He took a step forward, blocking the view of the camera and wiped them softly away. What a gentleman.

"It's okay, I'm here," he whispered.

"What about the rumors, they—"

"I don't care, you're more important than these stupid rumors."

Taking a deep breath, Jade nodded.

The boys started a group hug, waiting for them. All eyes were on them. Joonwoo waved them over to join. A small smile appeared on both of their lips before they jogged to them, joining the group hug. Screaming, "We love you, Yoon-Rae!" before walking off the stage made everyone at the ceremony tear up again.

***

"Will you be all right?"

"Everything will go like planned."

"You're worrying too much, Jade," Alex said, while passing them in the corridor.

"But what if you need something?"

"You know, there is this wonderful thing called a phone."

"Stop worrying so much. I got this."

"Are you sure, Hanjun?"

"Yes, I am."

"But—"

"The kids will be fine."

"I know, but—"

"There has to come a phase where the mother leaves the first time, and the father is alone," Tai added, walking past them.

"It's not that I'm concerned you'll do something bad. It's just, what if I miss something important?"

"Jade, nothing will be special before you come home."

Jade sighed again before lifting her head to see into Hanjun's eyes. They were honest and full of love.

"You have everything, right?"

"Yes, and if not, it will be at your house."

"You can call, and I'll come anytime, if there's something wrong."

"There won't be anything wrong."

"Mum, are you leaving already?" Dae-Jung stood at the edge of the stairs at the second floor, staring at them.

"Yes, DeeDee. You'll have some time alone with Daddy and your sister."

Dae-Jung ran down the stairs, into Jade's arms. His tiny arms were wrapped around Jade's neck when she stood up. Jade didn't say anything but hold him tightly.

"Okay, young man, that's enough for you. She still belongs to me. Come here," said Hanjun.

Jade chuckled and gave Dae-Jung a last kiss on the cheek.

"No, I want Mummy," Dae-Jung's finger reached for Jade's body, but Hanjun held him to his chest causing him to not touch Jade again. Jade's finger caressed Dae-Jung's face.

"Take care of Daddy and your sister."

Dae-Jung nodded with a smile. He hit Hanjun's shoulder slightly to guide him to put him down. Hanjun put him down and now caressed Jade's face. She looked up and faced Hanjun with a sigh.

"C'mon, I'll do great."

"I know, I just don't wanna leave right now."

"The earlier you leave, the earlier you'll be back."

"You're right. I think, I should just leave."

"I'll see you soon, Darling." Jade took her bag from the floor and got up.

Hanjun stood a few inches away from her. Jade could feel his breath on her neck before he planted gently a kiss on it. His hand went to her chin, lifting it up. Hanjun's lips made their way to her mouth, brushing her cheek and kissing the corner of the lips several times.

"Hanjun," she chuckled against his pecks. He smiled before pulling her in for a long kiss. His hand pulled her on her waist against him. Jade's phone start ringing, and they pulled apart. Jade fished her phone out of her bag. Hannah was calling.

"I have to go," she mumbled. "Take care, Darling," Hanjun whispered before he kissed her gently.

Hanjun guided Jade gently through the door and watched her walk down the driveway to her car.

After Yoon-Rae's death, the kids didn't have much of a problem with Jade and Hanjun. They accepted them really quick, and, for Jin-Ae, it wasn't it a problem at all. At the start, Dae-Jung had a little more problem accepting his father's death.

It's now five months after Yoon-Rae's death. While Jade worked a lot in their studio at home so she wouldn't be far away from Jin-Ae and Dae-Jung, after Yoon-Rae's funeral, Hanjun and the boys went to work to distract themselves a bit.

After two months, the partners of the members moved back to their own houses. All of them are still mourning the loss of him, but they try their best to live a normal life. It's still not easy for them. They knew Yoon-Rae for over twelve years. That's a long time.

Hannah tried to help Jade and Hanjun as much as possible and, of course, the members, too. Jade and Hanjun decided to stay at the mansion because Jade's house is still being renovated.

***

Hanjun had an argument with Jade late at night.

"Go! Just fucking leave!" she shouted at him.

He stared at her for a few seconds, clenching his jaw. "Fine," he mumbled.

Not having enough energy to fight back, he walked out of the kitchen, grabbing his coat and shut the door. Once he left, Jade turned the lights off downstairs, checked on the kids and crawled into the big, lonely bed.

'Yoon-Rae, I really miss you.'

'It's hard to live without you.'

'I hope, I'm doing a good job with Dae-Jung and Jin-Ae.'

'If you look at all of us, you can see we really miss you.'

'You know, since you left us, it was hard for everyone.'

'And, actually, it's hard to be a mother.'

'I think it's not easy for Hanjun either.'

'We argue more often, to be honest.'

'I'm scared I might lose him.'

'You know, he turned cold after you left.'
'He shut down any emotions he's had with the members.'
'He isn't the same anymore, although he warmed up again.'
'I miss you so much, Yoon-Rae.'

After a few hours, she woke up in the middle of the night. Jade walked down the stairs and noticed Hanjun sleeping on the couch. She frowned and looked away, but then she saw something out of the corner of her eye on the kitchen counter. Several small, beautiful bouquets of flowers, and there was a little note beside them. Jade picked it up and opened it.
Forgive me? :C
Jade's lips formed a smile.

***

Jade opened her eyes; the sun caressed her face and the bed behind her. She stretched herself and looked at her phone. 11:47, wow, that's late. Wait, actually too late for the children not to be awake.
She found no one in the kitchen, neither in the living room nor the dining room, when she heard voices outside the house. Jade turned around, opening the terrace door where she saw Hanjun playing with Dae-Jung in the grass while Jin-Ae slept next to them in the stroller without her making a sound.
Dae-Jung froze in his position when he saw Jade. "We woke up Mummy, Daddy." he whispered as if Jade couldn't hear them. Hanjun turned around with a smile.
"Sleep well, my sloth?"
Jade ran toward him, causing Hanjun to jump up and run away from her.
Dae-Jung sat down, looking at them chasing after each other.
"When I get you, you'll be dead."
"For that, you have to get me first, Love."
After a while, both collapsed on the grass, laying with their back on it staring at the sky.

Dae-Jung ran over to them, doing the same as them. Jade's breath went back to its normal status when Hanjun pulled her to him, causing her to be on top of him. "I just can't deny it. You look amazing on top of me." Jade hit him playfully.

"I can't wait to have you for myself one night.", he winked at her.

*** 

"I'll see you in three weeks, Darling,"

Hanjun kissed Jade before she kissed Jin-Ae and Dae- Jung.

"Take good care of your Daddy, all right?"

Dae-Jung nodded eagerly at her. She ran her hand through his hair causing him to pout at her. "Mummy."

"Don't act like that; I know you like it."

"I don't."

Kissing Jade for the last time, Hanjun waved at her. There she goes again to a concert week in Seoul.

Hanjun and Jade haven't found any maids who could look after the kids while they are at work or out of town, but they are working on it. Hanjun thinks when they move in together, maids would be a perfect solution.

# CHAPTER 11

"Jade, there you are." Junghoon closed the door behind him. Jade was currently in a hotel during her stay in Seoul. The staff and her bodyguards were all staying on the same floor, being near Jade but Hyunwoo wasn't with them this time. He had a personal matter at home that he needed to take care of.

"What are you doing here, Junghoon? I thought you would stay the week with your family."

"Something has happened."

"Why are you looking at me like that? What's wrong?"

"It's about Hyunwoo, Jade," he spoke, not looking at her.

Jade didn't move, she just stared at Junghoon. "What happened?" she asked, concerned.

'Please, just say, he is fine,' she thought.

He paused for a second. "He had a car crash, Jade."

"Wha—", she couldn't speak further; the words got stuck in her throat. "You have to be joking, right? You are joking. That's not true, right? Please, tell me you're joking, Junghoon."

Shaking his head, he stared at his feet.

Jade took one step backward, hitting the wall. Junghoon moved one step forward, approaching her. "I'm sorry, Jade. So sorry." He stretched his arms out to her to hug her, but Jade flinched away. "Please, don't touch me right now."

"Can I help you in any way?"

"I would like to be alone, Junghoon."

"Sure, just tell me if you need anything. Should I call Hanjun or—"

"I would like to be alone, Junghoon," she repeated herself.

"I'm so sorry, Jade."

She needs time alone, Junghoon knew that. But he was scared. Scared of her doing something to herself.

He is not just her boss.

He is also her friend.

A friend who doesn't want to lose her.

Knocking twice on the door, nothing was heard. According to the staff, Jade didn't leave her room for four days.

There she was again in the same hole she was after Yoon-Rae's death. He died six months ago but still Jade hasn't fully recovered from it. She acts like she had but she hasn't. She hasn't fully accepted his death yet. As much as she wishes, she just can't. Yoon-Rae had her trust, he could touch her and take care of her. The only thing she didn't let him see, is her broken self. She was too scared to might chase him away.

Well, Yoon-Rae knew she was broken, he could see it from the moment Jade came through the door if she had cried or not, but he never told Jade.

"Jade, I brought you food. You need to eat, remember."

"Could you open the door for me?", Junghoon asked softly.

There was silence. It was too silent, no way there is a human in there. But Jade had to be in there, she didn't leave the room. Junghoon tried over twenty minutes to get Jade to open the god damn door, but Jade didn't give a sound from her. Junghoon placed the plate on the table next to the door, pulling his phone out and after two rings, the call got accepted, "Please, I don't know what I should do. I need your help."

"You're here, finally." Junghoon stood up, almost running towards the person. The person looked to Junghoon as a sign for him to leave. Junghoon nodded, "Take good care of her, please", then he left. Leaving only the door between Jade and them.

The person knocked once at the big door, "Jade? Jade, it's me. Can I come in?"

There was no answer. The person tried several times but there was nothing. They got concerned, you could hear it in their voice. With another knock, their voice started being desperately, something Jade had only heard once before in their voice.

"Jade? Jade, c'mon, open the door. It's me. I just wanna see if you're okay. Let me in, please."

They couldn't open the door due the password, so they tried it over and over again.

Jade could hear them. They sounded really desperately and concerned but Jade doesn't want to see anyone. She wants to be alone, alone by herself. Not being touched by anyone.

She cried for hours, for days and didn't let anyone into the room. She was scared to face them, to hear their apologize for his death.

She doesn't wanna hear them.

She doesn't want to hear anyone.

She can't stand looking into their eyes and letting them see how broken she is, actually.

The first person who could touch and had her trust is dead.

Hyunwoo is dead, and no one could bring him back.

Jade could hear their knock loudly.

But she didn't want to open the door.

'What should I do, Yoon-Rae?'

'I can't live without him, too.'

'Why him?'

'What did he do to deserve this?'

'And, why me?'

'What have I done?'

Tasting the tears in her mouth, she stared down at the city lights. Talking to Yoon-Rae always calmed her down but today?

Jade put her earphones back in, closing the curtains of the window, not letting anyone see into her suite.

She sat down, staring at the paper stack. Reading them carefully one by one, letting her tears fall from her cheeks. She wrote several letters to Hyunwoo and what she wishes him.

Still listening to music on the loudest volume, she carried herself to bed, pressing a button to shut the outside world off, not letting any sound in her room not even Hanjun's voice, who still remains on the other side of the door.

She shut her phone off, not letting anyone contact her.

Pressing another button which lowered the blinds on her window. She put her earphones away, crawling under the blanket.

Hanjun still stood outside of her suite. He sat with his back to the door, his eyes closed. When he came to Seoul, he thought

Jade would open the door for him but eight hours later, he knew, Jade doesn't want to see anyone.

She doesn't want anyone to see her broken self again, but Hanjun saw it several times.

Why doesn't she want to let him see it? Let him help her?

"Mr. Kim? You're still here? I thought you already got into your suite."

"Did you forget the password, Mr. Kim?", a male hotel employee walked towards him with a towel on his arm.

Hanjun thought for a second, he smiled at him, standing up, "Yes, indeed."

"If I had a stressful day, I forget passwords easily." "That's no problem. I'll open the door to your suite for you. Let me search the password quickly."

Waiting for the hotel employee tipping things on his phone, he thanked him. With the phone in his hand, he walked to the big door of the suite.

"Here, Mr. Kim. The password is 130613."

"If you would forget it again, don't think twice and ask for help." "I will, thank you..." "I'm Sangcheol." "Thank you, Sangcheol."

Sangcheol bowed at him, Hanjun did the same before he tipped the password in. Making sure, the door opened with a click, Sanghoon walked away.

The door opened quietly, letting him in the room. He closed the door behind him. Taking his shoes off, not letting a single sound escape. Hanjun's eyes started to get use to the light, and he could see some bigger shadows.

Jade was awake. She was standing in the bathroom, watching herself in the mirror. She looked a bit thinner than usual, Hanjun guessed she didn't eat at all. Hanjun recognized his shirt on her, but Jade didn't move at all, she just stared at herself.

Hanjun jogged over to Jade, grabbing her waist pulling her into his tight grip, "Are you all right?"

Jade immediately pushed him away, "I'm fine, don't worry."

Hanjun was confused at her actions at first. He tried again, slowly.

"Hanjun, please. ... Don't touch me."

Instantly, his hand was near his body, away from hers, "You know, I'm here for you. You don't have to talk to me or anything. I'm just here for you."

Jade didn't look at him, but she did listen to him. As much as she didn't want to open up, she felt good hearing his voice. His voice was always so calm and had an effect on Jade.

He didn't say he was sorry, or it wouldn't be Jade's fault. Hanjun was just there for her and that's what Jade needs. Someone who is actually there for her.

Jade bit her lips before walking out of the bathroom, into her bed. Hanjun followed her with some distance, not wanting to push her.

Putting the blanket over her body, her eyes closed not making another move. Hanjun was sitting in the wing chair in the corner of the room, where he could watch over Jade and not going to her after she was asleep was the best he could have ever done. He knew, she would feel his touch on her, and he didn't want to make her uncomfortable.

Instead, he just stayed there, watching over her.

Jade slowly opened her eyes, her body hurts and asking for energy but she couldn't bring herself to eat. As her eyes got used to the darker light in the room, she saw Hanjun sitting on the wing chair. His eyes were closed, and his breathing sounded like he was asleep. Standing up quietly, she walked toward him. Gently, without a single sound, her fingers reached for his face. Caressing it carefully, she teared up again.

Hanjun could feel Jade's finger on his face, but he didn't open his eyes. Feeling her touch on his skin, gave him hope.

Hope that she won't lose herself again.

Hope that she will come back to him.

***

Bringing Jade finally back to their house after two days staying in the hotel without touching her, was a relief.

And still, he didn't touch Jade but when he's asleep-
he feels her touch on him.
Hanjun woke up, feeling arms wrapped around him. He lifted
his head, seeing Jade's tiny finger around his torso.
Why did she hug him? Touching him, she has no problem but
him touching her? Why did she let him touch her? Can he finally touch her again?
Taking a deep breath, he pulled Jade near him and she didn't
flinch at all, instead she snuggled herself in his chest.
His finger brushed through her hair as he smiled. A small smile
appeared also on Jade's lips. She finally let him touch her again.
Hanjun turned his head, looking to the baby phone, both kids
were asleep in their own room.
He turned back, inhaling Jade's scent.
Gosh, how much he missed that.

***

Finding Jade on the bathroom floor, staring blanky into space,
Hanjun approached her. His hands around her waist, pressing
her against his chest, he kissed her forehead.
Still in his embrace, he stood into the shower, holding her tightly.
Hanjun gently cleaned her body, then carefully shampooed her
hair.
"Sorry.", she mumbled in his embrace, holding the tears away.
"Don't be, Love. It'll pass."
"I promise."

***

Currently it's July...
To be exact, four months after Hyunwoo's death.
Jade misses him a lot.
She still talks to Yoon-Rae a lot. Talking with Yoon-Rae makes
her feel all right. She talks about everything with him ... her

struggles, her day, special things, new songs, the boys, her love life, the kids and Hyunwoo.

Her crying got less, but sometimes she still cries herself to sleep. After Hyunwoo's death, her nightmares about her father came back. She started to lose trust in anyone, even the boys. It was a hard way back to who she was before the accident.

And Hanjun? He didn't let anyone touch her without Jade's permission, neither the boys nor Junghoon, her boss.

Well, Jade doesn't know this, she still thinks the boys and Junghoon thought she was not ready to have them touching her, but the truth is they would love to hug her after this long time and for what happened. But Jade is afraid, and Hanjun won't let them.

It was another day and Jade had another argument with Hanjun about moving in together. Even though she loves the kids and Hanjun, she doesn't feel ready yet. It's complicated for her. Right now, it just doesn't feel right.

She yelled at him loud as fuck while Hanjun just sat there, looking at her. "Listen, you know what I feel for you and that I wanna marry you, have my own kids with you but—", he paused for a second. "You have to find a way to communicate your emotions without yelling at me. I'm not gonna have us arguing in front of our kids again, Love."

"I started this conversation, cause the kids are with Uncle Tai and not here."

"I don't want us arguing in front of them."

Taking a deep breath, she looked back at him. "Look, I know that you want to move in with me, but—"

"But what? I don't see any reason why not."

"You'll be so much at the work, and so will I be. I will come home in the middle of the night, and you will go early in the morning."

"That is the same thing we do every day. We come and go into the mansion. We talked about this before."

"Dae-Jung and Jin-Ae deserve a house with their family."

"I think, we're just not ready yet. I don't wanna be away from the kids so long, and you need to work as well."

"We talked about this, too and I shared my thoughts with you. I think we should get a maid or two, just for us and the kids."

"I don't know, Hanjun."

"What if we both search for a house, and if we found the perfect one, then it's our destiny, and we will move in together completely with maids and without any members? I mean we still have this dorm for all of us."

Jade nodded slightly with a small smile on her face. "All right, I give in."

Hanjun came toward her and kissed her forehead, "I love you."

# CHAPTER 12

It was already late, and the sky was in a deep purple tone with some clouds in it. The kids were already asleep in their beds upstairs.

Jade was already in the water near the stairs when Hanjun stood with his feet in the water.

"Don't come in the pool with your shirt on! Take your shirt off!" Hanjun chuckled and walked deeper into the water. "Don't say that," he said, while Jade walked deeper into the water.

Hanjun put his head in his shirt to check his body out when Jade walked to him. She shamelessly peeked also because she still couldn't see anything of his body yet. Jade went crazy after what she saw and put her hand over her mouth. Hanjun pulled her into a hug to let her feel every inch of him.

"Hey, stop it," she said in a higher voice.

Giving her a small kiss before letting her go, he walked a few steps backward. Jade observed him closely. He lifted his head and faced Jade again.

A small smirk appeared on his face when he slowly went underwater and Jade gasped.

He came up again, his hair wet, and you could see his body and his muscles through the wet shirt. The shirt laid tight on his muscular body. Hanjun rushed through his wet hair, looking up in her eyes. Jade stared in disbelief and put a hand over her eyes.

Removing her hand, he tried to hold his chuckle in. Jade looked into his eyes before they traveled down his body. One of her hands raised up as Jade glanced at him again. He just nodded, and her hands touched his chest. Her other hand joined her, and they traveled gently down to his abs. She touched them incredulously. Suddenly realizing what she had done, she put her hands back in a rush and took a few steps backward. "It's hard, right?" he asked, laughing. Jade chuckled and put her hands on her eyes.

Hanjun swam toward her, and pulled her back in. Bringing his hand up to her face, his lips met hers. One hand stayed at her waist, pulling her as near as possible.

Pulling away for fresh air, he didn't waste any second of it. He rushed back and bit on her lip to ask for permission so their tongues could meet. Jade granted him access, and they began to join in synch with each other.

Feeling his hands on her thighs, he lifted Jade up, her legs immediately wrapping around his waist, not letting any space between them.

Walking slowly forward, Jade's back hit the pool wall. She pressed Hanjun with her legs on herself, feeling something growing under her. His grip was tight, but it didn't hurt Jade in any way.

His lips, God—

Trailing down to her neck, sucking, and nipping on it. Tomorrow, there won't be a soft white skin. There will be art on it.

Noises coming from the terrace, she stopped Hanjun's movement, getting a groan from him.

Jade looked up, seeing Dae-Jung in the doorway not moving.

"Mummy, I can't sleep," he whispered tiredly.

"Aw, come little boy, wanna sleep with Mummy?"

Dae-Jung just nodded.

Jade pulled away from Hanjun, earning a loud groan from him. Receiving a peck from her, Jade turned away. "Maybe another day," she mumbled.

Picking him up, he waved at his daddy before they walked around the corner.

It is true; with kids comes less sex especially when there are no maids or babysitters.

*** 

"I have to go in a few minutes," Jade said while rushing back to the bathroom. "How do I look?"

She came back, wearing wide black trousers with a white loose shirt. Her hair was in low bun, and the black cap made the fit perfect.

166

"You look beautiful, as always."

"C'mon, don't lie."

"Darling, you do look perfect."

"And you'll get styled there anyway, don't worry."

"So?"

"Perfect for your dance practice later."

"Thank you," she said, kissing him on the cheek and then grabbing her bag.

"I'll be back after noon."

Hanjun kissed Jade gently before she almost ran down the driveway to her car. She has an important interview today, and there was a new schedule for a movie she'll appear in.

***

"Jade, I've missed you so much."

"I've missed you too, Sanghee."

Jade hugged Sanghee tightly before pulling away. She faced Joonwoo, smiling at him.

"Jade, how are you?" Joonwoo made a slight step toward her, but Hanjun walked up behind her, giving him **the look**, and Sanghee pulled him back by his wrist.

"No hugging, sweetheart. You know it," Sanghee mumbled before looking back at Jade.

Jade didn't think anything of it. She was watching Felix and Jae-Hwa talking with Dae-Jung while Dae-Eun, the youngest of Joonwoo's kids, played with Jin-Ae in her stroller.

Jade faced them again, smiling. "I'm good."

"And you Hanjun?" Sanghee asked.

"Well, we are up all night but not the way I would love it. The kids are the reason."

Jade playfully hit Hanjun on his big chest.

"Maybe we can change this for the weekend?" Sanghee took her shoes off before looking up again.

"I don't want you to watch them again. You already watched yesterday the whole day."

"Jade, I love your kids, and I have no problem watching them. Trust me."

Jade thought for a second before looking over to Hanjun.

"We can spend the weekend doing something different, if you want," he caressed her face gently, waiting for an answer.

"You can bring them anytime back at home, all right?"

"Perfect, you will see them on Sunday evening." Sanghee pulled Jade with her, leaving the entrance, and packing the things for the kids.

"I'm sorry about earlier. I didn't want to intimidate you," Hanjun said.

"It's okay, don't worry. I just didn't see Jade in person for a while. Sanghee always picked the kids up and brought them to us. I just forgot about the hugging," said Joonwoo.

"That's still doesn't give you permission."

"Hanjun, I got it. You're her overprotective boyfriend, and that's okay. She needs someone like you especially after the losses of her loved ones."

"She has no other men in her life who she's trusting right now. Not even her boss, don't let her forget how this is."

"Don't let her forget about the trust in men at least with you."

"I'm scared, Hyung. What if I won't make it? What if I'm not good for her or—"

"Hanjun, you were the one who got her back two times. Remember? After Yoon-Rae and after Hyunwoo. She trusts you with her whole life, and she loves you with her whole heart."

"Thank you, Joonwoo."

The boys stopped talking immediately upon hearing the girls walking downstairs chatting about manicure and hairstyles.

***

Jade woke up with her back to Hanjun's chest and his arms wrapped around her waist. She turned her body around so she's facing him but getting the sudden urge to use the bathroom, she tried and wriggled out of his hold only for it to become tighter.

"Five more minutes, Love.", he mutters resting his face into her neck.

"I need the toilet, Hanjun. Let me go."

"I said five more minutes, Love. Please.", he tightened his grip again.

"Hanjunnie-", she whispered into his ear.

"If you let me go, you can have a kiss."

His eyes shoot open, with a smile he unwrapped his arms from her waist.

Jade gave him a small peck on his lips before she stood up and walked past him to the door which is linked with the dressing room. She grabbed a pair of black panties and a bra before heading back to the bedroom to go to the bathroom which is linked with a door in the bedroom. It's absolutely amazing how many rooms actually are linked with each other and extremely practical. Jade looked over to the bed only to find Hanjun looking at her, "Turn around, I want to put the dirty clothes into the laundry basket."

"I'm not turning around, you're my future wife.", he crossed his arms and pushed out his chest trying to act dominant. Jade raised an eyebrow at him, "If you don't turn around, you're sleeping on the couch tonight."

His eyes grew wide with fear, he rolled his body around, so his back is facing her and let a groan out.

Taking off Hanjun's shirt and the black sweatpants she was wearing, she stood naked in the room. "Close your eyes, I'm walking past you."

Jade walked up to him, to see if he listened, and he did. He listened to Jade as if he is a trained puppy.

The water trickled down her body, washing off the soap. The glass doors began to steam up and the water got hotter. She drew a small heart on the door and smiled but a knock on the wall which separated the shower and the bathtub from the rest of the bathroom stopped her drawings. "Yeah?"

She heard him walking past the shower to the countertop and tried to cover up her naked body but realized the shower doors were already fogged up.

"Mind if I join?" Hanjun walked over to the shower.

"No," she replied, not thinking twice, and a few seconds later, the doors opened revealing a naked Hanjun. Jade's gaze moved, which she instantly regretted, a deep red blush covers her whole face and neck.

Hanjun slowly approached Jade, his eyes focused on hers.

Gently pushing his lips on hers, Jade moaned softly. Taking this opportunity, he plunged his tongue into her mouth, brushing against her tongue. The kiss became sloppy, the water still running down their body.

With one smooth motion, he lifted her up, wrapping her legs around his waist, pushing Jade against the shower wall, revealing her exposed body.

# CHAPTER 13

Jade turned her head to Hanjun. He just smiled at her, knowing she thinks the same. He squeezed her hand in his, before facing Ms. Park.

"What do you think about it? I did everything you told us and customized it with your ideal wishes. I really hope you like it." Jade stared at the big screen that showed their new home. It looked amazing, and the kids will love it. "It's perfect, Miss Park. Thank you so much."

Miss Park followed them to the door before saying goodbye. Jade and Hanjun just got the ideal house for them. After months of searching and discussing they finally found it.

Tomorrow will be the day that they'll have their own house. Although, several rooms on the fourth floor aren't finished yet. That was eight months ago.

Jade, Hanjun and the kids finally moved into their new house. The house was even bigger than their mansion in Pohang and, actually, it was almost a castle in which a queen and her king would live. Beside the castle size, it looks like a mafia mansion. They even have their own dance room, several studios, and a gym room. The unfinished rooms on the fourth floor, when they'd just moved in, are now perfectly done.

***

Jade walked up to Hanjun's studio and saw he was in deep concentration with the work he was doing. "Busy at work?" she casually asked, leaning on the doorframe with her arms crossed. He didn't even bother to look up as he only mumbled in agreement. It made Jade's eyes roll in annoyance.

Jade walked behind him as her hands snaked their way from his shoulders down to the chest. She inhaled his scent, missing it since the morning. "C'mon don't be too hard on yourself, Honey," Jade said.

Hanjun caressed her skin; she always liked it when he does that. "There's just too much, Darling. I promise to get this finished early and—" he slowly turned around and stumbled upon his next words. He was so busy with his work that he didn't notice the red lace set she was wearing.

"I went shopping with Hannah today, and I thought why not buy a set? Just for you," while she winked, she reached out to level her face with him, and her lips caught his.

"I should rest, definitely," he swiftly shut the laptop down and turned his chair around to face her as he wasted no time to pull her on his lap, his bulge hitting her perfectly.

Slowly untying the robe, holding her waist, kissing every inch from neck down to her chest, made Jade's stomach flutter in excitement and lust.

Looking into his eyes, the tension between them kept growing, and she couldn't take it anymore. Both of her hands behind his neck, pulling him in, her lips crashed onto his. Hanjun stroked her hair behind her ear, pressing her tighter to him. He was about to continue the kiss, when Hanjun's ringing phone interrupted them.

"Who is that?" Jade asked, as both of their heads turned to look at it. —**Joonwoo**—

Hanjun stared to the phone and back to Jade when she sighed, "I'll go."

Jade stood up, but Hanjun held her back by her wrist. She stared at him confused.

"Joonwoo? ... Can you wait for a second? I'll be right back," Hanjun muted himself and stood up. "Are you free tonight?"

"Why'd you ask?"

"Well, I wanna spoil you today. I would like to go out with you. No kids, no members, only us."

"We haven't done that in weeks," Jade's eyes lit up.

"I think we deserve this," he said.

"What time?"

"7 p.m.?"
"Sounds good."

Jade closed the fitting room behind her and walked through
the corridor to the stairs. Adjusting herself in the big mirror, a
smile was on her lips.
"Wow, look at Mummy. She looks stunning."
Jade smiled and walked downstairs. Her heels clicked on the
floor as she made her way down the stairs.
Hanjun stood up, brushing his suit smoothly, and admired Jade.
She looked really stunning in the red dress. It fitted her body
perfectly and showed all her features. The dress had spaghettis
straps and was a little tighter around her waist. It went down
to her ankles and was down there a little looser. A slit from the
bottom up to her thigh showed her right leg. She wore the ring
necklace Hanjun gave her, and on another finger, she wore another ring. It was the promise ring that Jade and Hanjun have.
Hanjun held out his hand for Jade to take. "My lady, ready for
our evening?"
"Always, my lord," Jade chuckled and made a little curtsy in
front of him as Hanjun bowed with his right hand on his chest.
"Mummy, where are you going?" Dae-Jung said, looking up to them.
"Hannah is coming over, DeeDee."
"And your Daddy will go out with your beautiful Mummy," Hanjun
replied with the biggest smile on his face.

"Are you cold?"
"Hm."
Hanjun took off his jacket, putting it over Jade's shoulders.
Giving her a tight back hug, he placed his head on her shoulder,
snuggling into her neck.
"Thank you, Hanjun."
"For what?"
"For this. I loved it. The evening was amazing," turning in his
arms, she stared into his eyes. Her hands caressed his face when
she leaned in to kiss him.

173

Pulling away, he rested his forehead on hers.

"I love you," she whispered quietly. A smile appeared on Hanjun's lips.

He gave her a passionate kiss, her hands wrapped around his neck, not leaving them once.

"I love you, Kim Hanjun."

"And I love you, Jade Evans-Kim."

What's going on? Is he proposing? Is he gonna ask her the question? Right now? Here?

Two and a half years were long enough to wait for Hanjun to pop the question. Going with Jade through thick and thin, losing a loved one, becoming parents of two kids …

So much weight has been on their shoulders and having a secret life without the fans knowing, he decided, it was time. Time to start a new chapter of their life.

Time to start again, without the bad memories of anything that happened in the last few years. But still, remembering every good memory over the years.

*\*\*\**

# CHAPTER 14

Some time has passed, and Jade released two movies this year. Jin-Ae is already three years old. Dae-Jung has grown to a tall boy and is already seven.

And Jade was right back then. Indeed, he is very smart. Going into the first grade, he spoke already two languages and wants to learn Japanese now, too.

Hanjun's and Jade's relationship didn't change at all. Still engaged, they want to marry once everything is settled down. They don't wanna rush, especially because they will do it all in secret. Hanjun was still the teasing and flirty guy he is, and Jade blushes at the simplest words. Being there for each other, helping each other, caring for each other. That's what their relationship is. But the life of a celebrity is hard. They don't want the press to know their relationship, and that's the hard part. They can't go out on dates that often or in public places.

For the schedules as an Idol or actress, the matching things have to stay at home, and for public meetings, they have to go as friends. In the company, they have to be careful.

Still in school, Jade has no time for him. Sometimes, she has so much to do for school and work that they don't see each other for the whole day. But still, they manage to do it.

*** 

Jade was studying in her room for her work she has to finish for the next day when Hanjun came into the room without a shirt.

"Hell no, what are you doing here?"

"What, am I not allowed to visit my future wife?"

"Bruh, and how am I supposed to study?"

Hanjun walked over to the big bed and laid in the middle of it, showing lots of his muscles while Jade was just staring at him.

"Take a picture, it will last longer."

"Oh God, c'mon. That's the most basic line I've ever heard."

"Don't lie, you've always liked them."

"Shut up. If you say one more offending thing, I'm gonna throw you out."

"I won't."

"I need to concentrate. Stay quiet."

"Sorry," he whispered.

Jade rolled her eyes, focusing back on her worksheet.

"Mummy, I can't sleep."

"Wanna sit with me?"

Dae-Jung nodded, climbing onto her lap, snuggling into her chest.

"He can bother you, but I can't?"

"Yes, Hanjun, because you are an adult, and he is a child."

"That is not fair."

"You love him more than me," he pouted.

"Are you really jealous of a kid?"

"I'm not jealous."

Patting Dae-Jung's back, she rolled her eyes. "Yeah, of course."

"I'm not jealous of a kid."

"Go on with your lies, I'm gonna study now."

"Love, have you finished?"

"No, I have not."

"When will you be done?"

"When I've written down everything."

"And how long will this take?"

"I don't know but if you bother me further, it will take much longer."

"Would you rather I stay quiet?"

"Yes, please."

"I thought you like it when I let it out."

Blushing at his words, she shook the dirty thoughts out of her head. "Maybe, but not in this situation right now," she mumbled. "Could you take Dae-Jung to bed?" she replied fast to forget what she just said.

Without another word, Hanjun stood up, taking Dae-Jung into his arms. "Let's go to bed, little wrecker," he whispered before leaving Jade alone.

Waiting for Hanjun to come back, Jade finally finished her study lessons. Uploading the documents, she shut down her computer. With the lights off, she closed the room, looking for Hanjun. Where was he? Did he go to bed?

He wasn't downstairs and neither outside.

Deciding to look in Dae-Jung's room, she found him next to Dae-Jung asleep.

\*\*\*

"I was asked to bring a date to the premiere in New York," Jade stated out of nowhere.

"Huh? I thought, that wouldn't matter."

"Well, it changed."

"Can't you just bring a friend?"

"I don't know."

"What about Alex? He is married, and he is your friend."

"As much as I love Alex, I'd rather go with you."

"Of course, I'm funnier, hotter, and sweeter than him."

"And you're also my fiancé."

"Not in public, Darling."

"Can't we just go as friends?"

"You sure you wanna risk it?"

"Daddy, buy ice cream?" Jin-Ae interrupted their conversation, running down the stairs.

"No running down the stairs, Sweetheart. You know the rules."

Thinking about the kids, Jade wasn't sure if she really wants to risk it. Their whole life could change if something bad happens.

"Ten minutes, Sweetheart. Mummy needs Daddy for a few minutes. Okay?"

Nodding her head, Jin-Ae walked upstairs, waiting for Hanjun.

# CHAPTER 15

"So, you need Daddy, huh?"

"Yah, shut up. That's not what I meant."

"You sure? Jin-Ae can go with Uncle Jae, you know?"

"I swear to God, Hanjun. Pull yourself together."

"Oh, now we are swearing to God?"

"Yah, we had a serious conversation here."

"This is also a serious conversation."

Rolling her eyes, she wanted to leave but Hanjun held her back, pulling her onto his lap. "I'm sorry, Love. Let's talk it out now, okay?"

Leaning her head on his shoulder, she almost teared up.

"Hey, it's okay. We will find a solution."

"I want to go with you but—"

"Then we will go together."

"But—"

"They know, we are really good friends."

"They will ask questions."

"And we will answer them as friends."

"What about Junghoon?"

"You can take either your boss with you or your hot fiancé. Your decision."

"I'll talk to him."

Kissing her softly, he went upstairs to take Jin-Ae with him.

***

"You look stunning, Darling."

Has Jade ever mentioned that she loves when Hanjun automatically speaks Korean as soon as they are out of South Korea? No? Well, yeah, she loves it.

They are on their way to the premiere of Jade's latest movie. The premier was held in New York, and while they are here, the kids are with Uncle Alex.

Opening the door, Hanjun got out first. He held his hand out for Jade to grab.

"Gentlemanly, huh?"

"All the time," he replied, chuckling. He closed the door behind her, leading her to the red carpet. The camera clicked as soon as Hanjun was out.

—Jade is not the only one who is famous.

Hearing their fans' screams, Jade walked up the red carpet, not leaving Hanjun's side once.

"Are you guys a couple?"

"Are you finally together?"

"Is there a future between you two?"

"When will we see you two together?"

They answered these questions all with the same answer. Then, they went inside after they took photos.

'I know. It's shocking but Jade didn't fall for my charms. Instead, she stayed friends with me,' was the answer that led Jade to chuckle the whole time.

"It's soon over," Hanjun whispered in her ear.

"Will there be another collaboration with you two?" a reporter caught their attention. Finally, a different question. "Or, with Jade and B'ONE?" he added.

"Unfortunately, there's nothing planned right now, no."

"That's a pity, you should be on stage soon, again."

"Well, we don't know what the future will bring."

"You have been off stage for so long. Why?"

"You can't stop your job just because someone died!" another reporter shouted.

"I—"

"What? You suddenly can't speak? Why's that?"

"Did you eat too many dogs or what?"

"Or, did you bring any other viruses with you?"

"The car is waiting, Jade," Hanjun interrupted, coming back to her. She stayed silent.

"Are you gay, or why are you wearing makeup?" he spoke to Hanjun. Hanjun ignored him, focusing on Jade.

"He doesn't even fucking understand me."

"Why is he here if he doesn't know a fucking word of English?"

"You mean for a man who learned English at the age of seven?"

"For someone who speaks more than one language?"

"Because I'm Asian and 'can't' speak the language you were raised with?"

"Because I don't look like I could speak the same language as you?"

"Because I'm wearing makeup, which makes me gay, but if someone of your race is doing it, it's powerful?"

"Because I'm more successful than you'd ever be?"

"Because I'm standing up against you right now?"

"Or, might it be, because I ignored your racist comments about Jade and Asian people?"

"What could it be, huh?" Hanjun replied calmly, without any curse words, and the reporter was too stunned to speak.

Never in his entire life has someone humiliated him in such a calm way. Hanjun was totally calm, not giving a fuck about the consequences there might be for speaking up in public to a reporter. If someone insults his fiancée, the fun ends.

Giving the reporters a smile, he turned back to Jade. "We have to go now."

Still bowing at the reporters, Jade walked with Hanjun to their car.

"Are you still mad, Love?"

"A bit, but I agree with your actions. Respect does go both ways."

"I'm sorry, Love."

"What if we get into another dating rumor because of that?"

"Friends would help each other out in such situation. And our company will fix it, don't worry."

"I don't want them to fix everything we failed on."

"I'm sorry. I didn't think before I act. I was just so pissed. No one can insult my fiancée," caressing her face, she looked up. "Let me make it up to you."

"Let me see if I have time for that," she replied with a smirk on her face. Actually opening her schedule plan, her smile faded away. "I'm sorry, but I think I have a bed date with my future husband."

"Do you think you know him?"

"I can show you, your future husband," pulling her on top of his lap, his hands traveled down her body while his lips leave everywhere kisses within a second after speaking up. Kissing her passionately, her hands gripped on his hair leading him to groan.

She started to unbuckle his belt when he stopped her movements. Shaking his head, he kissed her softly. "Today is about you, Love."

\*\*\*

Being back in South Korea, Hanjun's conversation with the reporters was everywhere.

The way he said it so smoothly and in a calm way without a curse word, leaving the fans assured that he didn't do anything bad. He told the truth. It's not okay to be racist toward any people. But, for an idol, you can't speak up to other people. Especially when you're not 'white'.

The company made him apologize for what he said.

The fans sent death threats to Dowoon, his manager, for making him apologize, but Hanjun went live then, clearing it up for the fans and to any other people.

"Please take my apology to note. I shouldn't have spoken like that. At that moment, I was just thinking about Jade and not the consequences. Please also don't say negative things about the reporter nor Jade. He apologized for talking like that. As I told the reporter, I do appreciate his apology. And again, I shouldn't have talked like that, and I apologize again."

\*\*\*

"Jade, you sure you don't want a cocktail?"

"I'm fine, but thank you, Sakura."

Sakura, Kai's fiancée, nodded, passing the cocktail over to Yu Yan.

The girls were having a girls' night while the boys were also out. Sadly, Sophia, Eric's wife, couldn't join. She is currently in France, filming a new movie.

Jade hadn't had such a great night in a long time, and she really needed it. The atmosphere was perfect, and everyone was having fun.

"**Wait**!" Jihoo screamed suddenly.

"Are you pregnant?!"

The girls' eyes widen, staring at Jade.

"No. Calm down. I'm not pregnant."

"Why aren't you drinking then?" Yu Yan raised an eyebrow with a smile on her lips.

"I'm not pregnant. I'm just a bit ill. I don't like to drink when I'm not feeling well."

"Are you sure you're okay?" Hannah whispered, a bit concerned. Is it really just an illness? Or is it more?

"Yeah, don't worry."

"Sprite?"

"Thank you, Mei Zhen."

"Cheers!" clinking the glasses together, Hannah and the girls hugged Jade tightly.

"It's so nice to be away from the boys and the kids for at least one night."

"Yeah, that's so true."

Talking about the others' lives, the time passed, and it was already midnight. They haven't had such a fun night in a long time. Jade was busy with the kids, her wedding planning, and her job, and the others had, of course, their kids and their jobs.

Hannah was also busy, not only in her work but also in her love life. Right now, everything works perfectly with both jobs, hers and Minwoo's and the thought of having kids is coming up.

Looking after Jade's kids, the thought grew and grew.

Opening the door of the mansion, the boys entered it.

"Look who's here, girls."

"Our men are back," Sakura said excited.

Hanjun smiled at Jade, not breaking the eye contact. Standing up from the couch, she made her way toward him. He was drunk. Fortunately, the kids were with Hanjun's parents.

"Helloooo, my Love," hugging her tightly, he took a deep breath of her parfum.

# CHAPTER 16

"Hello, Honey."

"I've missed you sooooo much, Love."

Chuckling at his words, she gave him a kiss on the cheek. "I've missed you, too, Hanjun."

The boys already took place next to their lovers while Jade still stood in front of Hanjun, "Let's go sit with the others, hm?"

Clutching onto Jade, his head rested on her shoulder, his lips almost touching her neck.

"Love?"

"You are mine, only mine."

Everybody heard it. And everybody laughed with a big smile.

"Yes, I'm yours, only yours, Hanjun," playing with his hair, she looked up, having everyone's eyes on her.

"So cute."

"You guys are really adorable."

\*\*\*

Jade grabbed her phone and quickly called Hannah.

"Yes, hello?" she answered.

"Can you come over? Quickly?!"

"Sure, what's wrong?"

"I'll tell you when you get there," Jade tried to calm her breathing.

"I'll be there in 20," she said, hanging up.

Jade looked down in her hand. The stick said —pregnant—

Hanjun was with the boys out for something important, thankfully. But, she was still stressing out.

She's pregnant. So it wasn't just an illness she had the other week. Her feeling was right.

She knows Hanjun wants to have a baby with her, but in the future. They don't have the time and energy for more kids right now. Dae-Jung and Jin-Ae are already exhausting, even though they're actually quite calm kids.

'What if he's not ready? What if he leaves me.'

'No, No, Jade, he loves you', she repeated those words over and over to herself.

"How do I tell him, Hannah?"

"Well, it doesn't have to be like in these romantic books or movies and stuff. It can be simple or extravagant. It's up to you, Sweetie. The important thing is he'll be happy no matter what," she reassured.

"I'm still scared, Hannah."

"You'll be a wonderful mother to your child. Look at you and the kids now. You're already doing awesome."

"Oh hey, girls," Kai greeted them, taking off his jacket.

"Hey," both mumbled. Hannah gave Jade an encouraging smile.

"Something wrong, my Love?" Hanjun asked, rushing toward her.

"No, everything is fine," Jade smiled up at him, trying her best not to break down.

Hanjun's eyes told her he does not believe this shit. "Let's go upstairs."

Hanjun cups her face in his hand, closing the door behind him with his foot. "Tell me, what's wrong, Darling. You look stressed."

Jade took a deep breath. If she doesn't tell him he's gonna keep asking questions.

"I'm pregnant," Jade mumbled. Tears were forming in her eyes, feeling him freeze.

"Wh-what?"

Is he mad? Will he leave her?

"Love" he whispered.

Jade shook her head, trying to get out of his hold.

"My Love, look at me, look."

She opened her eyes and saw a big smile on his lips, tears running down his face.

185

Jade felt like a huge weight had lifted off her shoulders.

"I'm happy, okay? I'm so fucking happy we are having a baby!" picking her up, she wrapped her legs around his waist.

Jade looked at him and saw him still crying. Wiping his tears away, she gave him a kiss.

"Were you worrying I wasn't going to be happy?" he whispered against her neck.

"Y-yeah, Dae-Jung and Jin-Ae, they both need so much time, and I know, we talked about kids in our future, and I thought you weren't going to be happy for it because of our jobs—"

He shook his head. "With you, I'm always ready. Ready for everything. We need to decide where the nursery is going to be, a name, buy clothes! Oh, and—"

Jade shut him up with a kiss. "We have time for that, months, to be exact."

"I'm just so excited! A baby!" he smiled and kissed her again.

***

"Jade, which cocktail do you want?"

"Oh, I'm not drinking, but thanks."

Drawing the attention to Jade's and Eric's conversation, everyone listened.

"Wait—", looking between Jade and Hanjun, his mouth dropped. "Are you—"

Nodding, Hanjun pulled her softly in. "Yes, I'm pregnant."

"Oh my God! Congratulations!" Eric squeezed her tightly before hugging Hanjun. The boys followed.

"For how long?"

"Almost five months."

Telling the members was a scary and big step.

Hanjun and Jade are indeed scared. Scared, how it will affect their job.

What will happen after birth?

What if someone finds out about it? Should they publish it? Shouldn't the fans know about it?

All that and the fact that they're having their own child is the scary part.

Hanjun's family was told shortly after they found out she was pregnant. Next were Junghoon and Dowoon. They were happy for them, but warned them about the consequences it could bring with it. And soon after, Jade contacted Jake and her mother. Then it was time to tell the members.

***

"We are on our way, Si-woo."

"Yes, the cake is in the trunk."

"I have to hang up now. See you soon," hanging up the phone, Jade looked through the window at the streetlights.

Everything happened really fast.

Jade was looking out of the window, and, while she turned her head, she could feel Hanjun's hand on her chest, pressing her against the seat.

Hearing her name one last time, everything went black.

# CHAPTER 17

Hanjun sat there, not looking at anyone, praying everything will go well.

It can't be true. Why is it happening? Why Jade? What did she do to go through this? What did they do to go through this? First Yoon-Rae, then Hyunwoo and now ...She has never done something wrong to deserve this. To go through such a hard surgery. One that decides if she will live or not.

On their way to Si-woo and Malee, they had a car accident. Someone crashed into them, and as hard as the truth is, the driver didn't have much damage, but the passenger didn't have such good luck.

And Jade didn't have as much luck as Hanjun. Hanjun had a few scratches and some bruises on his body, but Jade— She is still in surgery after eight hours.

The nurses couldn't tell Hanjun much. He just has to wait.

After he had his round check, Hanjun informed the boys and Hannah.

Within an hour, all were there, praying for Jade and the kid to survive.

While the boys and Hannah waited outside the room, Hanjun was inside another one to be alone.

He broke down, with so many tears falling down his cheeks. He already cried for two hours straight. Hannah was with him then but now, no one was.

Hanjun started punching the wall, not giving a fuck. His wife is in a situation not even the devil wants to be. And his kid— it has to survive. She can't die. She has to survive.

Their kid is their hope. She can't die in there. And Jade can't die either. Both have to survive.

Coming out of the room, he sat back next to Yijoon, his sister, holding her hand tightly. His whole family is with them right now: his brother, sister, father, and mother. The partners of the members joined them after Jade's fourth hour in surgery.

"Mr. Kim, the doctor would like to speak to you," a nurse appeared, trying to smile for him.

"Did she make it? What is with our kid? Is everything alright?"

"Please, Mr. Kim, come with me," leaving him without an answer, Hanjun followed the nurse nervously.

She knocked twice on the door before opening it. The doctor turned around and, to be honest, he didn't look happy. He didn't look good either. He was tired and definitely not very happy.

What happened with Jade and the kid? Why doesn't he seem pleased?

"Did they make it?"

"Mr. Kim—"

"Your kid—"

"No, please—" Hanjun sat down on the chair next to him, trying to catch his breath.

"I couldn't save her, Mr. Kim," the doctor lowered his head.

"Mrs. Evans-Kim lost a huge amount of blood on the way to the hospital and, in the accident, she hit her belly somewhere that almost killed the baby, but then due to blood loss, the baby didn't make it."

"I'm so sorry, Mr. Kim. I did everything I could."

"Is Jade alive? Is my wife alive, Doctor?" Hanjun started to panic. The doctor didn't tell him anything yet about Jade— what if she didn't make it either?

"She is stable but still unconscious. She will wake up in a few days, don't worry."

Hanjun took a deep breath. She made it. Jade is alive. But their Sunshine—

"She lost much blood, and, when she wakes up, she will need you, Mr. Kim, her husband. You will both need each other. I'm very sorry for your loss, Mr. Kim. Please, excuse me now," the doctor bowed at Hanjun respectfully before he left the room. The nurse followed him, leaving Hanjun alone.

He started yelling loud as fuck while Joonwoo appeared in the door frame, seeing him so desperate. "Hanjun!"

**"Calm down, please!"**

"Get out, Joonwoo."

Closing the door, Joonwoo approached him.

"Please stop, this is not your fault."

**"I said let go!"** Hanjun pushed Joonwoo to the floor. He stared at him in shock.

"I ... I didn't mean to h-hurt you I—"

Joonwoo looked up into his eyes, "Didn't mean to hurt me?"

"Jade lost your child in this accident, **someone else caused!** Not **YOU**, not **HER**. It was an **UNKNOWN** person who was probably drunk, Hanjun!!"

"I don't know what to do," he whispered. "She is as hurt as I am, and, right now, she doesn't even know she lost her. I disappointed her in being a good father. She lost our baby, and I can't face her because I feel **bad** ... I feel so bad, Hyung. I ... I don't know what to say anymore."

"You need to calm down, Hanjun. You can't get another panic attack. Jade is in the room next to us. She needs you, okay?"

"It is all my fault. If I would have done bett—"

"You **have** done amazing. You **were** the best. You **are** the best. You couldn't do better than this, but at the moment, you're doing **shit**. And shit doesn't help. Jade needs you. Even if she's unconscious right now, as soon as she's awake, she'll need you."

Joonwoo saw Hanjun's hands shaking. He knows he will soon have a panic attack.

The shaking hands weren't that bad, and he knew he could help him with it, but as soon as the breathing starts, Joonwoo knows, it will be hard to calm him down again.

"I... Hyung, I can't brea—"

"Hanjun, please."

It's there. The ragged breathing arrived and soon — Hanjun threw Joonwoo on the ground. Yes, the outburst due to sensory overload.

**"No, I... I can't—"**

"Hanjun, DON'T"

Taking a chair, Hanjun smashed it on the wall, "**I hate myself**."

Standing up again, Joonwoo hugged him tightly, not letting him go, "I'm here for you, Hanjun. We all are but what Jade needs is you. Her future husband, alright? She needs you the most of all."

Talking to him for almost thirty minutes, his breathing got calmer.

Pulling away, he had tears in his eyes. "I'm gonna be waiting outside. No one is in her room. Talk to her. You need each other right now."

Hanjun stayed silent.

"I'll give you a minute," Joonwoo walked through the door in the other room in which Jade was.

*The nurse who brought Hanjun to the doctor informed Hannah, the members and his family about Jade and the baby. Joonwoo immediately went to Hanjun, but he had already started to break down. That was right before Joonwoo was pushed to the floor by Hanjun.*

Joonwoo knows how he feels. How it feels to lose a child. Sanghee and he lost their second child during the birth of their daughter. Jae-Hwa would have been the third kid and Dae-Eun would have never existed.

The family let Joonwoo go, all of them knew what he went through and that it would be the best when he goes.

How will Jade react after she'll find out?

She loves kids, and she wishes nothing more than to have her own next to Dae-Jung and Jin- Ae. She will be devastated.

Hesitantly, he took a seat next to Jade. His heart shivers when he sees her. Hanjun locked his hand in hers as he watched her. Kissing her forehead gently, he closed his eyes, staying like that for a few seconds.

Tears fell down on the pillowcase. He just wants her to wake up now. To be with her. To cry together. To mourn together. Just not to be lonely. His other hand rested on her leg, feeling the warmth of her body. Hanjun didn't move for two days, he neither drank nor ate anything. He just watched her.

Joonwoo opened the door with Dae-Jung and Jin-Ae. Hanjun was in the same position as he was yesterday. The boys were already here an hour ago to visit Jade and Hanjun.

Jade's mother and Jake were both informed, but sadly they won't come. They decided to leave them alone, not wanting to disturb them. Well, that's what they said, but Hanjun thinks they just don't want to help. It's not like they don't appreciate Jade, but like yeah, they only appreciate her and not actually being there for her when she needs them. Not even when she loses her baby and is still unconscious.

Dae-Jung and Jin-Ae just stood there, staring at their mum laying in the bed with all these machines around her. Dae-Jung gripped onto Joonwoo's hand tightly while Jin-Ae couldn't bear to look at her mum; she turned her head away from the sight of her injured mum.

Hanjun smiled softly at his kids, not wanting to scare them away. His eyes were red and puffy. Looks like he cried the whole night. He turned his head back to Jade when he saw Jade slowly gaining consciousness.

"Love?" he said as she slowly opened her eyes. Dae-Jung saw it and started smiling and pressed Joonwoo's hand out of joy.

The doctor started taking her vitals as she gained full consciousness. He's adjusting the drip as Jade turned to Hanjun. However, her focus is interrupted as she puts her hand to her stomach and looked down at it. He saw her eyes starting to fill with fear and tears.

"My child ... WHERE'S MY CHILD?!" she yelled, holding onto her stomach.

"I'm so sorry, Mrs. Evans-Kim, but we, I couldn't save her," the doctor said. He spoke to her in English, not wanting her brain to overwork right now after this shock.

"What do you mean by 'COULDN'T SAVE HER'?" she screamed. **"Where is my child?!"** she yelled again. Feeling a bit dizzy, she ignored it completely.

Joonwoo immediately lifted Jin-Ae on his arm, holding onto Dae-Jung's hand tighter and leading both out of the room. "Let's give Mummy and Daddy some space, huh?"

Closing the door behind him, he heard Hanjun speaking to Jade.

"Love, listen to me," Hanjun said trying to calm her down.

"No! Please, this can't be true!" she yelled, taking the drip out of her hand and removing the blanket off her body. Hanjun held her back onto the bed as she screamed and yelled more.

A gush of pain filled his heart at this sight. She cried in pain for her child as she held her stomach. "Our child—" her voice broke as she cried laying her head on his chest. Hanjun wiped his tears away as he held her close to his chest.

"Our child is gone, Hanjun," her voice was desperate. Hanjun pulled Jade's head from his chest and wiped her tears away. "She will always be remembered, Love."

Kissing her forehead, Hanjun saw the tears rushing down her cheeks again.

"Hyung, I don't know what to do. I don't know how I can help her—"

"Hanjun, you don't need to do anything else."

"But—"

"Be there for her. That's everything she needs."

Looking into Sanghoon's eyes, all he saw was honesty and the truth. Jade doesn't need anything more than him. Not his talk, nor his encouragement. She needs **him**, her fiancé.

Snuggling into her neck, Jade was already asleep when Hanjun joined her.

She is still under supervision. The accident happened a week ago, but her health was already much better.

QY Entertainment released an article about the car accident and how it will go on. Hanjun and Jade's name were both mentioned in the article leaving the fans not unknown about what happened. Although Hanjun only hurt his arm in the accident, he won't take part in the dancing at the annual awards show in September. The doctor said it would be too risky to perform with it.

***

Discharged one day before the awards show, the doctor wanted to see Jade again the next day.

For the time that Jade was in the hospital, the kids were living with their Grandparents, Hae-Won and Seo-Jun.

"Hello, Mrs. Evans-Kim."

Bowing slightly at him, he patted at the examination table next to him. "First, we are gonna do a round check."

Nodding, she laid back and relaxed all her muscles.

"In a few weeks, you can start to exercise again. Slowly. You can't play around with a car accident and definitely not with a still-birth, Mrs. Evans-Kim. Do you understand?"

Nodding again, they got interrupted by a knock. "Yes?"

"Mr. Kim is here, Doctor."

Hanjun appeared at the door, smiling at Jade.

"Hello, Doctor," walking over, he kissed Jade gently, sitting down next to her. "I'm sorry for being late. We were just practicing for the awards show."

"No problem, Mr. Kim. It's good that you're here now."

"After you woke up, Mrs. Evans-Kim—"

"Please, call me Jade."

"After you woke up, Jade, I made another round check, and might I ask you something?"

"Sure."

"Did you have an abusive childhood, Jade?"

Gripping Hanjun's hand tightly, he stroked her thumb, looking into her eyes. "It's okay, Love," his lips formed. Turning back to the doctor, his eyes locked with hers. "Yes, I had an abusive childhood, Doc," she whispered, hesitantly.

"Might I ask for how long?"

"It started at the age of ten."

"Could you tell me about it?"

Taking a deep breath, Hanjun brushed her arm slightly, assuring her, he's right behind her.

"My father is alcoholic ..." she started her story.

Telling the doctor was hard for Jade. Even after all these years, it will never be forgotten. She just can't forget what he did to her. What they did to her. What she, herself, did to her.

"That explains a lot," the doctor mumbled.

"But why is this important, Doc?" Jade looked up again.

"Look, Jade, you've been through a lot, no wonder you're hurt," he paused for a second. "I wasn't sure until you confirmed it, but— Even if you hadn't had this car accident— There is a 90% chance you would have lost your child."

"What?" both replied, shocked.

"There is a study about miscarriage and a woman's abusive childhood. Childhood adversities were associated with miscarriage in this study, and, after what you told me, you had a really bad and abusive childhood. Of course, I can't diagnose 100%, but there's a high chance you would have lost her."

"What about future kids?" she asked, nervously.

"If I look at your past and this accident, the possibility of a rainbow child is more low than high, but there is still a chance of you getting pregnant again and giving birth to a healthy child. I don't want you to believe you'll never be able to have a child, but I have to warn you about the possibility of it not surviving."

Hanjun pressed Jade's hand tightly, not letting her go.

"However, in my opinion, as big as that loss would be, nothing can be worse than not trying it again," the doctor added, with a small smile. "I wish you two only the best. Please, excuse me now," leaving Hanjun and Jade alone in the room. Jade teared up.

"Hanjun—"

"It's okay, Love. Everything will be good."

"We will find a way."

"But—"

Pulling her in, she wrapped her hands around his torso and didn't let him go.


Later that day, Hanjun had to leave for the awards show.

Jade was alone, no one was with her.

Hanjun didn't feel good about leaving her alone, but he couldn't do anything about it. Jade barely spoke to him throughout the day. Neither did she smile after the appointment with the doctor. Well, of course, it's heartbreaking what he told them, but throughout the years they've spent with each other, both know that the best thing is when they talk. Hiding their feelings from their partner has always ended badly.

# CHAPTER 18

Closing the door behind his back, Hanjun heard a sound from the living room.

Was Jade still up?

Checking the time on his phone, he was confused. Yes, Jade is a night owl but not if she has to work the next day. Why is she still up? Normally she would already be in bed.

Approaching Jade, he saw her lying on the couch. A blanket over her body, her head on a pillow. She was asleep. Hanjun was relieved seeing her like this. Better like that than being still up. Lifting her up, Jade snuggled herself into his chest.

"You've been through so much, Love. You don't deserve this," his words came out as a whisper, letting her drift off to sleep.

Checking her wrists, nothing has changed. A relieved sigh left his mouth.

He is right. For Jade, the last few years haven't been easy.

Of course, she had great memories too, but the others will never not leave her soul, mind, and heart.

Losing Yoon-Rae was one of them. It didn't seem real to her. She couldn't accept his death. Whatever she tried, she just couldn't. And then Hyunwoo. Her best friend and the one she trusted first. Losing him, she couldn't put that loss into words. But actually, she accepted his death earlier than Yoon-Rae's. Maybe it was because he died involuntarily, in an accident. Hyunwoo may have let her down by leaving her, but it wasn't on purpose. He didn't plan to leave her. But after all, she can't be mad at Yoon-Rae. Well, actually, she was never mad at him for leaving her. She was shocked and couldn't believe it. That was the hard part of accepting his death.

Yoon-Rae knew that Jade could go on without his help; she just couldn't see it back then.

And now? Yeah, she is happily together with the love of her life but her future of having kids? The kid she just lost days ago?

She feels miserable. She feels disgusted. She feels everything other than loved.

She just won't let the words of the doctor stay in her head: 'There is a chance you can get pregnant and give birth to a healthy kid.' She feels like a mistake. She can't give Hanjun what he wants the most.

But he doesn't care about those things. He doesn't need kids from Jade (and himself) to be happy with Jade. He needs only Jade, and, right now, that's almost impossible. Even for him.

It's hard, and she's really gone through a lot. She just doesn't see it. Doesn't see that she's been through a lot.

***

"Would you like some tea, Love?"

"I'm good."

"Do you want anything to eat?"

"Hanjun, I said, I'm good."

"But—"

"I said, I'm good. How many times do I have to repeat myself?"

"I just want you to feel all right, Love. I care about you."

"Why? Why do you fucking care about me, Hanjun?"

"I have nothing left."

"I'm broken and also lost your kid. Hanjun, I'm not worthy of it." Grabbing Jade's arm, she turned back around. "What? Do you want to lie to my face that I actually have something left not to be ashamed of?"

"How many times do I have to tell you to believe me? How many times until you finally see what I see in you?"

"Don't lie to my face," she shook his hand off. "I've lost your kid. I brought you bad rumors. I'm just a hurdle for you. I don't bring you happiness, I bring you bad luck."

"Jade, stop this shit right now! I'm engaged to you because I love you. I chose you because **you** make me happy. I love you for who you are. I'm not disappointed in you, and I could never be." Taking her arm again, his grip got a bit tighter.

"When do all these lies stop, Hanjun?" sighing, she looked into his eyes. "I'm sick of your lies, Hanjun."

"I'm not—"

"I can see the disappointment in your eyes. And don't tell me I'm wrong. You are disappointed."

"Jade—"

"No, I don't need anything from you. Just tell me I'm right. Tell me you're disappointed in me," not breaking the eye contact. Jade pulled her arm fully back. "I guess you can't even do that. I'm done here."

Walking past him, she felt the tears in her eyes.

"Jade, wait!"

Running after her, she was almost in her car.

"Yes, okay. I'm disappointed! Is it that what you want to hear so desperately?" his words made Jade stop. He finally confessed it. He's sick of her.

"Yes, Jade. I am disappointed. I'm so fucking disappointed in you. I thought you could do better. I thought it would get better but no— It only got worse," his voice got louder.

# CHAPTER 19

Jade just stood there. She wasn't looking at Hanjun. She didn't move at all. The door of the car was still open when the sky suddenly got louder.

Soon after, people were running into their houses.

Jade didn't. Neither did Hanjun. Both just stood there, at least ten meters away from each other.

"I thought it would end and the disappointment would fade away, but it didn't. You are right, Jade. Why did I lie right to your face all these years I've spent with you because you're nothing than a broken wreck, right? Why did I go through all that effort when I'm disappointed in you, right? How could I love you with all the depression you have. How could I actually consider marrying you with this disappointment. I know, how stupid can I be, right?"

"Is it that what you want to hear? Because then I would be telling lies! Jade, I would be telling lies," his voice almost broke completely.

Turning around, her face was completely covered with tears and the rain left her in drenched clothes. Not feeling the cold on her skin, her hands balled into fists. "Why are you still lying after all we've gone through? Hanjun, I just don't see what you see in me. Please, just stop all the lying. I don't want to hear them anymore."

"I'm **not** disappointed in you for losing our child, Jade. I'm **not** disappointed in you for having a hard childhood. For having such bad influence at a young age. For losing your loved one. For going through several therapy sessions. And neither am I disappointed in the mother you are for our kids."

"**Stop lying!** I know you're disappointed," Jade's voice got louder, and so did Hanjun's.

"You know what?"

"Yes, I AM disappointed in you. So fucking disappointed."

Jade broke down. Her knees gave in, and she fell to the floor.

He rushed over to help her up.

"Do not touch me."

"Jade, look at me."

Slowly turning her head to him, her body started shivering. Hanjun noticed it. Of course, even when they fight, he always noticed when something happens with Jade. Taking off his hoodie, he offered it to Jade. Well, he ordered her to wear it.

"I'm disappointed that you don't see your true self. The one I fell in love with. What she's gone through or what she actually wants in her life. That you still don't want to see through me how much you've grown. That's what's disappointing."

"It's disappointing because I thought you would see it through me. But you didn't."

"I'm **not** disappointed in you, Jade. Not at all. I'm more disappointed in me for not being a good fiancé, a good friend, a good lover." His grip around her shoulders loosens, and although it was hard to see through the rain, Jade could see the tears in his eyes.

"I just can't, Hanjun," her words came out as a whisper. "I can't do this right now. I'm sorry. I need some time for me," kissing him softly before hugging him for the last time, she got into her car, leaving him all alone by himself in the rain.

She left.

She really left.

***

'I miss you, Yoon-Rae.'

'And I need you.'

'I can't be alone in this world.'

'Hyunwoo isn't here either.'

'And I had a big fight with Hanjun. A really big one,' leaning her head at the wall next to her, the door opened.

"Hey," his voice was soft. "Can I bring you something? A cup of coffee? Tea? Water?"

"Thank you, Minwoo but I'm fine."

"Are you sure?"

"Yeah, and thank you for letting me stay for so long already."

"Jade, you're like my sister. Even when Hannah isn't here, you're always welcome."

"Thank you, Minwoo. Really."

Hannah was currently in Paris on her world tour. Yes, world tour.

The concerts in America were the first part. Europe's next, and then Asian is the end of it.

"Do you want to talk about it?"

Sighing out loud, she turned her face to the window. "I had a big fight with Hanjun. We're kinda on a break right now."

Minwoo couldn't speak. Hanjun and Jade on a break? The perfect couple on a break? The fight had to be really big if they are on a break.

Minwoo could somehow feel that Jade didn't actually want to talk about it.

"Listen, go take a shower, and I will cook something. You must be starving."

"I'm fi—"

"I didn't ask, Jade."

"I'll bring you some of Hannah's clothes," and without giving her time to respond, he already closed the door behind him.

It's already been two months, and Jade still hadn't talked to Hanjun since the fight.

While Hanjun still tried to talk with her about what happened, she shut off completely.

She needs time for herself. And Hanjun finally understood it after two weeks.

She needs time to move forward, to heal and even though he wants to help her, this time—

he can't. She needs to do this on her own.

Not trying to approach her at work, he knew where she was staying through the fight. At Hannah's and Minwoo's house. He is glad Minwoo was able to help her out in this kind of situation.

"Thank you for the meal, Minwoo," she thanked him, bringing the dishes to the kitchen.

"Anytime, Jade."

"Are you heading somewhere?"

"Yeah, my friends want to go drinking somewhere. Would you like to join?"

"Uh, I don't think it would be all right."

"C'mon, Jade. You haven't been out for two months. Let me treat you."

In the end, Jade agreed to join. He is right, she hasn't been out in more than two months. She also hasn't seen her kids since then. And, she really missed them.

"Jade, your phone has been ringing for almost a minute, you should check it," one of Minwoo's friends handed her the phone.

—**my handsome man<3**—

She immediately closed her phone. They shouldn't know about her relationship.

Jade disagreed with Hanjun to change his name into something cute. She was scared someone would accidentally see it and confront her. Seems like he did it anyway. Accepting the call, she didn't speak.

"Love—", his voice sounded desperate.

"I miss you."

"I really miss you so much."

"I'm so sorry about what happened. I shouldn't—"

"It's late. I'm gonna hang up," she interrupted him coldly.

"Love, wait—"

But it was too late; she had already hung up.

Hanjun couldn't believe it. After leaving her alone for two months, he can't do it anymore. The kids are asking questions and soon they will know she isn't actually on a business trip for inspiration nor in England with her family.

The boys are still trying to distract him and the kids, but for him, it doesn't really work. At least it works for the kids.

Telling his members goodnight, he walked upstairs without another word.

'What have I done wrong, Yoon-Rae?'

'Why doesn't she come back?'

Tasting his own tears, he wiped them away, forcing himself to take a shower before going to bed. He tried for so long to understand her, to wait for her, but it is harder than he thought it would be.

*** 

Holding the beers in his hand, he heard the boys' voices on the terrace.
"Have you heard from Jade?"
"Sanghee tried to talk with her, but she said Jade was busy."
"Malee tried, too. She was also busy."
Hearing Hanjun, they changed the topic as if nothing happened.

Jae hit Alex slightly, turning his attention to his.
"What?" he mumbled.
Jae didn't speak up, his eyes stared down the aisle. Alex let out a small sight before following his eyes when he almost dropped his beer.
"It's time, Hanjun."
"See ya tomorrow."
The boys were suddenly all upstairs, leaving Hanjun confused and alone.
"What the hell—"
Checking the time, it was time to go to bed. They were right but why didn't they just say it?
Hearing a noise, he turned around and actually dropped his beer. Yes, this time, he let it fall.

She was here.
"Jade—" he couldn't speak further. Jade already threw herself into his arms. Without a second, she started to let everything out. He needs to know it. He needs to know how much Jade missed him. How much she regrets staying away, suffering alone.

Staring out the window, Jade took a deep breath.

'Yoon-Rae, what should I do? I miss him so much.'

'Do you really think he is not disappointed in me? That he still loves me?'

'Please, give me a sign. Anything,' waiting for something to happen, she closed the window.

He wasn't responding anyway. But suddenly, the wind opened the window again.

"What the—"

"Yoon-Rae?" Jade rushed to the window, opening it fully, stepping outside the room.

In the wind, leaves are flying, doing some sort of dance together. Jade couldn't believe it. This has to be a sign from Yoon-Rae.

'Should I try it again? Should we try it again, Yoon-Rae?'

'Give me another sign. Is it worth trying it again?' but the wind didn't respond. The leaves weren't flying anymore. Nothing was heard.

'I guess not then.'

Kneeling down, she leaned her head on the wall behind her.

'It was a bad idea anyway; it probably wouldn't even work out.'

Closing her eyes slowly, she heard a noise. She didn't bother opening them again, but suddenly the wind was back.

'What? What do you want Yoon-Rae?'

'You made it clear. It's not worth it.'

But it didn't stop. It got worse, and the sky opened up.

Rain was everywhere, and all the leaves left except two. They didn't leave. They stayed, dancing in the rain together.

It was the sign. The sign of love. Even the rain couldn't stop the leaves from dancing together. Their love was bigger than to just go home. They did what they wanted. They wanted to dance right now, and nothing would stop them.

Maybe Jade needs to look at her problem like the leaves do. Not bothering if anybody stares, if anybody talks, or what happened in the past. To look into the bright future she could have. To look into Hanjun's eyes, seeing nothing but love. Yoon-Rae gave her the sign. She knew what she has to do.'

Looking back up again, Jade brushed his tears away, kissing his cheek gently.

"I've missed you so much, Jade. Don't do this ever again. I can't handle this alone. I need you, Jade. I love you, Jade," his voice sounded weak and desperate. He is telling the truth.

"Why aren't you talking? Have I said something wrong? Please, speak—" his words got stuck in his throat.

A small smile appeared on Jade's lips while brushing Hanjun's hair out of his face.

"What?"

Taking a deep breath, she locked eye contact with him. "I thought about us and—"

"Please, don't. Please, I'll do everything you want. Just–"

Stopping his talking with a small kiss, his grip around Jade tightens a bit.

Jade pulled away, staring into his eyes again. "I wanna try it again, Hanjun."

## ~ THE END ~

# The author

Seraina Schrag was born in Sursee, Switzerland, and is still living in the country. She loves to read, write and sing. She especially loves playing percussion and singing.
This is her first book.